"This is a propulsive, harrowing, and ultimately ennobling book. Kathleen Kilcup has been to the abyss and back, and her writing shines with the grace of one who knows she's been saved. 'God's truth is life,' wrote Patrick Kavanagh, 'even the grotesque shapes of its foulest fire.' Kilcup has suffered some of those shapes. The miracle—and it does seem that—is that she has emerged with God's other, higher kind of fire."

—**Christian Wiman,** author of *My Bright Abyss*

"Kilcup's debut defies easy characterization: It's a coming-of-age chronicle, a military memoir, a story of addiction, and a spiritual quest. Poetry and God are Kilcup's two most constant companions on her winding journey to sobriety and a kind of personal peace accord. As I read, troubling news reports clamored for my attention and anger. And yet Kilcup held me rapt and filled my heart with compassion for all on similar journeys."

—**Kayla Williams,** author of *Love My Rifle More Than You*

"At once an orison and an odyssey, *Between the Light and Me* captures the edges of our fallen world with striking clarity. Kathleen Kilcup establishes herself here as a top-end writer, seeking and wise, and her meditations on faith, recovery, and military service deserve wide readership."

—**Matt Gallagher,** author of *Daybreak*

"This memoir is both devastating and gorgeous. Kilcup tells an unflinching story of longing, both for God and for human connection, and the human frailty—what the author calls *sin*—that gets in the way. I savored every sentence, delighted in every page, and readers will too."

—**Joanna Eleftheriou,** author of *This Way Back*

"Here's a life that refuses to lie down in defeat—a life of drama, complexity, and challenge. *Between the Light and Me* is not only exceedingly intelligent, it is spiritually moving. Reading it, you will be challenged and grateful, giving glory to God."

—†**Luci Shaw,** author of *Reversing Entropy*

"Recalling the loose and desperate writing group that formed among her military peers while she was serving in the army, Kathleen Kilcup writes, 'They wrote about limbs blown from bodies; I wrote about God. And somehow we knew we were all writing about the same thing.' As its subtitle suggests, *Between the Light and Me* traces the porous boundary between beauty and violence in our messy, blessed human experience. Kilcup's memoir does not flinch from a candid record and does not dishonor the difficult details of her disoriented and at times self-destructive story by prettying them up, but rather patiently sits with the hard episodes out of a manifest faith that they, too, are beautiful, though that designation may require a divine re-evaluation of what constitutes beauty. The result is a narrative in which holiness settles into the mundane, the vulgar (in both senses of those terms)—which is indeed the very principle of the sacramental, and specifically of the eucharistic. Kilcup's brave telling argues that life—real, unperfect life—is not a shame that holiness must fast from but rather *food for the journey*."

—**Kimberly Johnson,** author of *Fatal* and *Uncommon Prayer*

# Between the Light and Me

*a memoir of beauty and violence*

•

Kathleen Kilcup

Here Below Books
*grand rapids, michigan*

Here Below Books is an imprint of
Wm. B. Eerdmans Publishing Co.
2006 44th Street SE, Grand Rapids, MI 49508
herebelowbooks.com


Published 2026

Printed in the United States of America

32 31 30 29 28 27 26 1 2 3 4 5 6 7

ISBN 978-0-8028-8527-2

**Library of Congress Cataloging-in-Publication Data**

Names: Kilcup, Kathleen, 1983– author
Title: Between the light and me : a memoir of beauty and violence / Kathleen Kilcup.
Description: Grand Rapids, Michigan : William B. Eerdmans Publishing Company, [2026] | Summary: "A spiritual autobiography that traces one woman's search for God as she wrestles with violence, addiction, and depression"— Provided by publisher.
Identifiers: LCCN 2025029654 | ISBN 9780802885272 hardcover | ISBN 9781467469821 epub
Subjects: LCSH: Kilcup, Kathleen, 1983– | Christian biography—United States | LCGFT: Autobiographies
Classification: LCC BR1725.K4858 A3 2026
LC record available at https://lccn.loc.gov/2025029654

*To Graham*

# Contents

# A Note to Readers

This book is a memoir. It's a memoir in the sense that everything you are about to read is a truthful rendering of my memory. But memory, even when vivid, is colored by both perceptual gifts and shortcomings. This is not a journalistic account of my past but an honest portrayal of events through the lens of limited consciousness.

Also, it should be said that this story makes use of traditional literary devices. Years are compressed. Whole dimensions of experience are omitted. Names are changed. Dialogue is reconstructed to resemble but not replicate actual conversations. Perhaps most painfully, there are people who love me and whom I love who make no appearance in the pages that follow. And the people who do appear are necessarily distorted by the art of the book. This book is what it must be: a slice of life held up to the light, examined, and then hewn into something called story.

Thank you for reading.

# Preface

My four-year-old son is obsessed with the ocean, but only a very specific part of it, the midnight zone. The ocean is stratified into five layers. There's the sunlight zone, the twilight zone, the midnight zone, where darkness dominates and the few creatures who live there are strange—where a snow of dead flesh falls without ceasing. Below midnight comes the abyss. Then, the trenches.

I am glad he isn't interested in the abyss yet, though he may be soon. For now, he shows me pictures of vampire squid and siphonophores, deep-sea dragonfish, and the fangtooth. But there is one creature that has captured my imagination more than any of the others: the football angler.

It is a black fish, oil slick, and in the shape of a prolate spheroid—a football. Above its head hangs a kind of grotesque fishing pole, at the end of which is a small, bioluminescent bulb. The fish uses the light as a lure. It spends most of its time waiting in a dark and empty sea, except for the endless curtain of falling flesh-snow. When a smaller fish unwittingly draws near to the light, the angler explodes into a sudden feeding frenzy. Then the small fish is gone, and the angler resumes its waiting in the dark.

In the midnight zone, creatures are deformed by darkness and pressure—or so it seems to me. The aesthetics of the deep sea are terrifying and cruel. For me, it is a place of compressed evil—a place so barren and brutal almost nothing beautiful can survive.

There are places like this all over the world—human places and wild places, though more often we live in twilight. For a time, I lived in a midnight zone. A place of pressure and lightlessness. What I mean to say is, this is a story about being human, born into a violent world and carrying violence inside ourselves—and in that darkness, how hungry we grow for light.

In many ways, there is nothing special about my story. We all have our versions of it—suffering, moral failure, spiritual deformity. There are endless examples in the blighted world of desires gone askew. But this is the story that was given to me, the only story I really know how to tell. It is a story about a girl who loved God but did not know how to bend her will to his. You've heard this story before. She was drowning, and then a great fish swallowed her.

# Violence, noun

*Synonym: ambivalence of the human heart (see: Jonah)*

1. swift and intense force:

    [The ball of his foot against stone as he
    turned away]

2. rough or injurious physical force, action, or treatment:

    [A storm nearly capsizing the boat]

3. an unjust or unwarranted exertion of force or power, as against rights or laws:

    [The sea swallowing a man]

4. a violent act or proceeding:

    [A fish swallowing a man]

5. rough or immoderate vehemence, as of feeling or language:

    [A prayer leaving the throat of a man, leaving
    the throat of a fish, leaving the sea]

6. damage through distortion or unwarranted alteration:

    [The confusion of one kind of death
    with another]

*There interposed a Fly –*

*With Blue - uncertain - stumbling Buzz -*
*Between the light - and me -*
*And then the Windows failed - and then*
*I could not see to see -*

Emily Dickinson,
"I heard a Fly buzz - when I died -" (591)

*You cannot conceive, nor can I, of the appalling strangeness of the mercy of God.*

Graham Greene, *Brighton Rock*

I

# Eugene, Oregon

*Thunderheads gathering at the rear*
*abyss of things,*
*lightning, quick swizzle sticks, troubling the dark in-between.*
*You're everything that I'm not, they think,*
*I'll fly away, Lord, I'll fly away.*

Charles Wright, "Looking Around"

The church was red. Or, at least that's how I remember it. A small adobe building with a blue onion dome tucked in among dripping trees on Blair Boulevard. Everything drips in Eugene. Wet clouds are pushed by Pacific winds into mountains that trace a north–south line along the Willamette Valley; then they drop south and sit in great, gray glops over Eugene. Whole months of gray and wet. The sky, not a sky, but a soaked cotton ball.

Against the gray and flat light and dark northern greens, the church rebelled. *Bright*, it said. *Feast of color.* Maybe that was some small part of the reason I found myself sitting outside the doors late one evening, a soft mist of rain falling. I think I might have cried there, but maybe I just sat and looked at the doors, believing, somewhat self-pityingly, that I could not cross that threshold—that fate and circumstance had conspired to press me to the outer edges of God's love.

A small, elderly Orthodox priest (though maybe he was only fifty then) must have seen me from the window of his house next door.

He came out and sighed and asked if I'd like some tea. He did not seem pleased to extend the invitation, but I followed him into the yellow light of his living room, where his wife set out a glass teapot, inside of which bloomed a beautiful pink tea flower. I had never seen anything like it. So delicate and fragrant and at odds with the colorless isolation I had felt outside.

We chatted awkwardly for a few minutes. What could I say to these pleasant and good people about my life? The drinking and self-loathing and poverty and failure? The pervasive and self-confirming sense that I simply did not belong in the world?

My stuttering silence led the priest to furrow his long, caterpillar eyebrows. Then he pulled out an album that chronicled the church's history. *See?* he said, his glasses reflecting light. *Before it was a church it had been a chicken hatchery, then a tofu factory, and then a building owned and nearly destroyed by anarchists.* When the church purchased the building back in the '90s, it was covered in graffiti. There had been symbols of devil worship, pentacles and the sign of Lucifer. I nodded politely while he shared the vaguely interesting story with me and then thanked them for the tea and said that I had to be going—though I had nowhere to go.

•

For months afterward I drank tea out of a giant plastic yellow cup. The tea was cheap and herbal, and I filled the cup half full of almond milk and Splenda. I liked the way the yellow cup looked in my hand as I stood at the giant living room windows looking out over a sea of milky fog and pine. Crows swung silently around branches, their black bodies stark and swift against pale clouds.

I lived in the living room of a house I shared with three other women. All of us were poor, but I was the poorest. A few times I traded food stamps for rent, and then I would walk down to Whole Foods or Sundance, a fancy local grocery store. Rich people get things for free, and so, as long as I didn't look homeless, I could eat by sampling the hot soup and cheese and bits of fruit. Sometimes I stole food outright. Like the time I picked up a loaf of bread and walked out the door; or when, at a gas station, I filled a cup with cheap, sugary coffee and then walked up to the counter where I pretended I'd left my wallet at home. The clerk comped me the coffee. I knew he would. I didn't look like a thief. I didn't sound like a thief. But I was.

•

It was 2009. The world was still reeling in the wake of the 2008 market crash, a fact that meant very little to me except that suddenly I found myself at twenty-five, a recent college graduate and Army veteran, in the unemployment building, sitting next to women who had advanced degrees in things like marketing and chemistry. I occasionally peeked over at other women's computer screens to see what sort of jobs they were applying to and realized with a sense of doom that we were all aiming at the same secretarial positions.

I didn't come from poverty. Both of my parents were the first in their families to go to college—and both eventually became professors. Dad had earned a PhD in intellectual history from Harvard back in the '60s. Mom would eventually earn a PhD, too, though later, after long stints wiping baby bottoms and working part-time gigs to help make ends meet. No, we weren't poor. We were idealists, which might be worse. It meant that financial and practical realities always took a back seat to the grand internal work of thinking.

The mortgage was a nuisance. Clothing, cleaning, and the clock were distractions from the lofty, atemporal thought plane. Although my parents never explicitly said so, we grew up thinking that most conventions of normal, civilized life were a little beneath us. And so my younger brother, Henry, and I were almost never on time for school. We showed up fifteen minutes late, disheveled, our homework half done and crumpled at the bottom of our backpacks.

I'm not sure any of our teachers or classmates got the memo about our superiority. My parents must have kept that secret pretty well guarded. All of which is some part of the reason that, in 2009, it didn't bother me very much to find myself wearing the same unwashed blue sweater day after day. And though I didn't like the feeling of precarity that came from unemployment, a part of it felt right to me. I remember sitting on a bench outside Whole Foods watching paying customers cross over the threshold into the warm, plant-filled, lavender-scented interior. From the smell of wet pavement outside to bright citrus and organic bathing salts inside. Order, beauty, health. And I thought, if one of these dumb jerks would just accidentally drop a twenty-dollar bill, they'd never notice, but it would change my whole life. No one did. I just sat there in my grime and self-pity, feeling morally superior to all the pleasantly dressed working folk who had their eyes on the last bag of organic cotton candy grapes.

•

I had lost my job as a barista after showing up drunk to work one morning. Or was it was because I slept with my boss's brother? Or maybe it was because I wasn't actually a very good barista.

I really did *want* to do a good job. I'm pretty sure I gave it everything I had. But apparently what I had wasn't much. Even when I tried to do everything right, I always seemed to mix up the almond and oat milks or forget to write something down or leave a bagel in the oven too long. One day, long before I got fired, I came in from taking out the trash, and my boss looked at me and said, *I get the feeling you want to be somewhere else. It's like you're always dreaming.* I stared at her for a minute before saying something rambling and confused about how much I did want the job.

And I did. It sucked, frankly, to try to do a simple job and fail. I wanted to whip out fancy drinks and have appropriately brief chats with customers. But too often I seemed to startle awake from a dream. My boss would catch me staring at the weird pattern of light reflecting off the display case. Or she'd sigh and look pointedly at the clock because I took twice as long as anyone else to sweep the front room. And I was always surprised to look up and realize that I had been sweeping somewhat artfully, with large, lovely swooping motions that were almost useless for gathering up crumbs.

So when she fired me, I suppose it should not have been surprising. And yet it was. A lot surprised me back then. I did not see what I didn't want to see and then was shocked when the unseen somehow, unjustly, forced itself into view.

It was that way with Will. Before the blue sweater took up a more permanent residence on my torso, before I lost the job at the coffee shop, I had a sometimes-boyfriend. Thirteen years older than I, Will was a little ashamed of me and a little in love with me, while I was completely and insanely devoted to him. He was a playwright and taught at a small, private college and had me over to his apartment and toasted bread for me in his oven and talked about Dante and Kierkegaard. At night, when I couldn't sleep, I'd crawl out of his bed and lie on the cold linoleum floor and watch the watery moonlight make strange and desperate patterns through tree branches against his wall, and I felt something like kinship with either the branches or the light, I didn't know which.

Will was athletic and wide-shouldered. He looked more natural on a basketball court than in front of a classroom. He was sweaty and unsure and tried to cover up what he didn't know with questions or charm. But I didn't like to see that. What I liked instead was how much he liked me. I also preferred not to think about what it might mean that I was consistently attracted to older, professor-type men. I didn't like to think about that at all.

Once, we biked along the Willamette River at night to a little pub, where we ate calamari and drank too much pale beer. And then, later, back in the summer night, he pulled me off the path toward the riverbank and kissed me and said it was like kissing strawberries and cream. It seemed like a terribly romantic thing to say, even though I kept picturing him trying to kiss a bowl of whipped cream and how messy it would be with cream up his nose, and I wasn't sure I liked to be compared to that kind of thing.

It was spring and then summer, and so I often walked the mile or so to his apartment. When I left the Army some two years earlier, I had been given a flask that I carried in my purse as I walked. I took little sips of screwdriver as I kicked pebbles and let the wind between my knees and looked around at brightly flowered yards and old stonework and painted doors and broken sidewalks with bouldering tufts of grass and sometimes birds and the rare blue sky open overhead. Walking and looking around were two of my favorite things. And drinking.

I'm not sure how conscious I was of *needing* something to drink in order to be around Will. But I almost always drank before seeing him and insisted that we drink when we were together. It did not seem possible to me to be both attracted to someone and sober around him. Sobriety and vulnerability seemed an acid mix, the sort of thing that leads to skin peeling off. That was the feeling of it. But with just a little gin behind my eye, I could hide all that naked flesh.

There was something about the solidity of Will's frame and the essential goodness I sensed underneath his fear. Something like the kinship I felt with either branch or moon. Or somehow both. And it was that, perhaps, that I hoped he could sense in me, too.

The other thing, besides sex and booze and literature and philosophy and the vague sense that our relationship was a little taboo, was that he, like me, was a Christian.

•

Christian. Poor word. Once the fiery name of martyrs, mystics, women wandering the desert. It was a word that kept company with other words, beautiful words, like thirst and burning and holy. A person cannot look at God and survive—but for Christ—and so a Christian was a person who, with fear and trembling, looked at what cannot be seen. But what is the word today? It wears pastels, I think, and eats cookies after church services that evoke intense but somewhat opaque feelings of warmth and security.

I was raised in such a church, and as soon as I was allowed, I shucked the old sheep's skin—that's what it seemed to me, complacency and cowardice and dullness of mind and spirit. I dyed my hair an awful shade of blue, proclaiming to my parents, who honestly weren't at all dismayed by my rebellion, that I didn't believe in the virgin birth; I didn't believe in resurrection from the dead; and I was forthwith 100 percent uninterested in church. I think I was fifteen.

In part, the problem was that the church we attended was not in any way prepared—neither liturgically nor pastorally—to address anything like the deep and socially unacceptable hungers I felt. It seemed a place for nice people, and though I was unfamiliar with the interior lives of the parishioners at Ascension Lutheran Church, I felt that I was not like them. I did not especially care about being nice. Instead I wanted—with all the fervent idealism of an untested teenager—something real and painful and beautiful, the mystery underneath the mystery. I wanted the truth. And, perhaps to my credit, I did not sense it in the soft NPR voices coming from the pulpit, reminding me again and again how little is required of Christians, how easy and mild and frankly likable Christ is. I wanted none of it.

•

French philosopher Simone Weil has a wonderful line: "A beautiful woman looking at her image in the mirror may very well believe the image is herself. An ugly woman knows it is not." I remember standing naked in front of a full-length mirror when I was young—already conscious of my ugliness, already aware of how both children and adults seemed to hate me for it, and I was confused. I knew that I was larger than most girls, that my thighs and arms and face were thicker, softer, that clothes sat oddly on my shoulders, that my eyes were pale and framed by blonde, nearly invisible lashes. But I also knew in the deep, inarticulate center of myself that I was beautiful because of the life I was, the fire God had lit in me and kept burning, hour after hour. I was furious that the world could not see how beautifully he'd made me. I'd been cast out. A religion that could only conceive of the outcast abstractly ("the homeless," "the marginalized," "the other") was a poor religion. There I was in a pew week after week, hoping for something real to speak into the pain of my life. But pain was not the subject of Sunday sermons. Reassurance was. The people suffering were *out there*. Both God and man, it seemed to me, became washed-out, thin versions of themselves.

I didn't stay ugly. Nor did I keep that angry distance from the church for long. I'd become a Christian, but a strange one, full of longing and sin. Imagine a girl in her twenties at a Mediterranean-themed bar. Belly dancers undulate under orange light in a corner. She's on her third rum and Diet Coke when she begins chatting up the boy standing next to her. When she learns he's a Christian, her whole body goes electric. As though the church were a secret club, she feels this young man must know about her anguish and her deepest loves, and by the time she's had three or four more drinks (Malibu and orange juice, then vodka Redbull) she is unable to hear, through the blood in her head and the joyful glowing stars outside and dreamy fluidity of beauties trembling past them as they walked home, that he was not that kind of Christian at all.

•

By the time I met Will, I'd been a devoted, though recklessly sinful, Christian for many years. I'd read somewhere about the left-handed way to God—the way through shadows, then darkness. I'd misunderstood Saint John of the Cross's "dark night of the soul," thinking that there was more truth, or a harder truth, to be had in the lightless regions. Truth by way of ruin—by way of drunkenness and shame and an intimacy with sin that would make a more pious sort of Christian blanch.

Will, I think, wanted to be that pious kind of Christian. Or, at least he wanted to be like his dad, who was that sort of Christian. But he also wanted to write plays and hang out with theater people and drink like an artist and hurt like one. And so, we gave that to each other—hurting one another with sin and loving to be hurt that way and also grieving it.

When he broke up with me for good, we were sitting on my bed. He held me while I cried pathetically into his shoulder and begged him not to go. And even though some part of me had seen it coming and that same part of me knew it was right for him to leave, the louder and hungrier part of me, the part that could never be satisfied or loved enough, took over. That, I think, was a mercy—the beginning of a certain kind of end.

•

After Will broke up with me, I nose-dived. I went to parties and tried to amass evidence that I was lovable. There were plenty of drunk boys willing to play the part of evidence. But the feel of it all was off—tinny, like the echo of a song that reminded me of something. None of the boys were exciting enough. The adventure wasn't big enough, bright enough. None of it worked quite right. Not the booze or the boys or the coke. My despair had outgrown my drugs.

I started making breakfast smoothies out of rum and frozen strawberries and almond milk. Then, for ten days I didn't eat—a cleanse, I said. My Sri Lankan friend, a brilliant woman who was studying for her MA in English at the local state university, agreed to shave my head with a Bic razor when I asked. My mother cried when she saw me. My brother called it my Britney Spears moment.

Being bald was its own kind of rebuke. Will had loved my hair, and I'd loved that he loved it. And so the logic was that if I could shun the part of me that had made me desirable, I could shun desire. I'd wanted to put away vanity. Except when I did, I did not become less attached to my looks. I was not above it all. I was just, infuriatingly, bald and vain.

Vain and bald and skinny and drunk.

In that state, I arrived one October evening at a bar in downtown Eugene. Here's what I remember: I ran into an ex, a sallow-skinned kid I'd dated just after moving to Eugene. He was not a great guy. Once, I told him I was afraid of snakes. The next week he took me to a pet shop in the mall and pressed my face against a glass terrarium filled with snakes. I'd screamed, but he kept my face pressed there until I stopped squirming.

I don't know how it unfolded exactly, except that on this October night we wound up back at his apartment, and what I did not want to happen did—against my explicit and vocal will.

The next morning, I walked home in the early morning rain. If there was light, I don't remember it. I walked the wet streets. Four miles home. My bald head had become a sign of every shame I had inflicted upon myself.

I probably slept when I got home. (Now I can imagine with such gentleness how the light might have found my resting cheek.) After waking and eating two fried eggs, I called my little brother. He was one of the sanest people I knew, though I wasn't sure why or how he'd become that way. There was a time when we'd gone head-to-head in the self-destruction department.

But that twenty-two-year-old boy picked up the phone and listened to his hungover sister cry about her tormented life and then said with totally uncharacteristic tenderness that maybe I should go to a recovery meeting for alcoholics to see if I could relate. Half hopeful, half scoffing, I said, *You think* I'm *an alcoholic?* I was sure I wasn't. I was sure my problems were much more complicated and deeply rooted and ultimately unsolvable than that.

•

Like most American churches, Orthodox churches in the US often print weekly bulletins with pictures on the front. But in the Orthodox Church, those images are almost always reprints of famous icons: Saint George on a white horse, his spear hovering above the head of a black serpentine dragon; Saint Mary of Egypt with tangled, dirty hair and weather-beaten skin acquired after forty wandering years in the desert; the Theophany: a scene of Christ immersed in the Jordan, the water drawing back from him in awe, fish and strange underwater creatures staring at the inscrutable mystery of God's baptism, the descent of the dove, the voice of the Father represented by a scroll unfurling in the sky.

Orthodox art did not embrace the three-dimensional turn taken by its western counterpart. Not because there's anything wrong with three-dimensional representation but because iconography, that specifically ancient Christian form of art that is also prayer, does not aim at realism but at reality—the life that inheres in and is expressed by every holy, living thing. Icons are interested in depicting not just a human face, but a human face lit up by the heart-piecing joy of life-in-Christ. The geometry is flat. Lines are dark and defined. Shapes are somehow more real because of their total disinterest in appearing real. Gold and blue, sand, water. The saints' eyes are not dreamily canted up toward clouds but often stare, without a hint of a people-pleasing wink or smile, directly into the viewers' eyes, as though challenging them with the stakes. Death, remember?

In those days, I couldn't afford real wood-mounted or painted icons, so I cut out the paper reprints and taped them on the wall next to my bed. There was one of Jonah and the whale. Another of Saint Anthony fighting demons in the desert. At night, before falling asleep, my little red prayer book collecting dust on the box I used for a nightstand, I would look at those icons and sort of press my mind into them, like I wanted to fall straight into the scene. What a relief it would have been to have that kind of clarity. Here are the demons, I could say to myself if I were in Saint Anthony's place. And I could fight them in the dust of the road and swing a stick, and maybe, like the great saint, I would be overcome by them. But the battle line would have been drawn, and I would have known where to aim.

Then one night as I lay lost in morose thought, orangey lamplight cast up and around the two embattled saints, a thought suddenly occurred to me. *You're in the whale.* What I needed was dark ink. Draw the stomach first. The scene. The smell of salt water and rot. It wasn't much, but it was all the honesty I could afford.

•

The first time I set foot in a recovery meeting, I walked straight to the back row and hunched over. I saw a coffee maker on a counter and small Styrofoam cups. Up front a large blonde woman wearing a black leather jacket was talking, and though I don't remember most of what she said, I do remember with incredible clarity how plainly and honestly she spoke about things that would have sent me into convulsions of shame. And then she laughed. And everyone laughed with her.

Later, a bearded man announced that they would pass a basket to collect money for the meeting and that no one was required to contribute. That was good because I had no money. He also mentioned that anyone who needed it could take a dollar out.

It was fall then. I was in the stinky blue sweater phase. It rained all the time. After the meeting, I darted quickly out the door and felt the cool spatter against my head.

## 2

# Ft. Leonard Wood, Missouri

*It seems to me I am trying to tell you a dream—making a vain attempt, because no relation of a dream can convey the dream-sensation, that commingling of absurdity, surprise, and bewilderment in a tremor of struggling revolt, that notion of being captured.*

Joseph Conrad, *The Heart of Darkness*

They're supposed to get you ready to die. That's the goal—not dying but becoming willing to die. I was eighteen, naive and hungry and, yes, willing. In basic training, I don't think they particularly care what skills you acquire. Nine weeks isn't a lot of time to learn how to navigate in the woods or shoot or throw a grenade. But you can learn to suffer. In nine weeks, if the conditions are right, you can learn to empty your head and fill it with fear and reflex so that when the time comes you do not care whether you are running into machine-gun fire or sending a mortar to a house filled with children.

Drill sergeants weren't allowed to hit or use actual swear words anymore. But the goal was the same: "Break them down. Build them up." And that was why, on so many mornings, they made us stand for hours in shorts and T-shirts in February's freezing dark. We could not stamp our feet or rub our bare arms, so sometimes ice hung from our nostrils by the time we were released. It's why drill sergeants screamed, spit flying from their purpled lips, anytime a shoelace was untied or someone wore the wrong sock or a bed wasn't perfectly made, and the whole company was then taken to the tire-scrap pit and made to exercise long past the point of muscle failure—long past the point of pain and collapse. And it's why we never knew what was coming next; why I started sleepwalking to my locker, where I somehow found my Kevlar helmet and put it on and then, still asleep, marched up and down the hallways until a friend would gently lead me back to bed. Later, when I was supposed to be guarding a foxhole in the middle of the night, I fell briefly asleep, and in my sleep I picked up a shovel and beat that same friend. When I woke we cried together.

Any of it could have been an adventure. But it wasn't. Or it wasn't the kind of adventure an eighteen-year-old imagines from her couch while watching an "Army of One" commercial. A girl's hip bone cracked open on a ruck march. We took turns walking into a dark gas chamber where we were shrieked at by furious men and told to remove our gas masks and breathe in poisonous air. And then we ran from the chamber gasping for breath, red-eyed and half-blind, long strings of snot hanging from our noses. On Sundays, when the drill sergeants might have been home with their families or at bars getting drunk, some of us took turns sleeping on the cold tiled shower floors we were supposed to scrub, knowing that if we were caught everyone would suffer. When our drill sergeants yelled, *What makes the green grass grow?* we screeched back: *Blood! Blood, Drill Sergeant!* And then we barked insanely as we stabbed rubber dummies with bayonets.

See what I mean? No one uses bayonets anymore. They weren't teaching us skills so much as they were indoctrinating us into a world of radical obedience. Servile. Undignified. Evil. But that's what war is—what it requires.

One day, we were practicing hand-to-hand combat. In those days, they taught Brazilian jujitsu. I was paired with a girl a little smaller than me, and soon I had her pinned. And then she started wailing. Her leg was bent where it should have been straight, at the shin. She was hauled away, and we never saw her again. That evening, during dinner in the chow hall, a drill sergeant approached me in front of everyone and in a loud voice offered me an ice cream bar. *Kilcup!* He shouted at me. *You a killer now.* It was a compliment. My name, up to that point, had been Little Orphan Annie because of my short, red hair. Every time I made an error, the drill sergeant would sing "The sun will come up tomorrow . . ." as the whole platoon was worked over in the pit. But from that day forward I was Killer.

It was an absurd name, and everyone knew it. I was about as far from a killer as they come. I'd naively wanted adventure and difficulty, but not the obliteration of human dignity. I felt like vomiting after the girl's leg broke, and when it was time to scream about blood I couldn't muster the volume or enthusiasm they wanted. I was mocked for it and punished.

It's not that I was more moral than anyone else. There were plenty of other kids there who hated that stuff (and plenty who didn't mind and some who liked it). But I was stubborn and sensitive and easily horrified. My imagination built out our training—put flesh on it. We were not just playing at death; we were getting ready. What was to some more pragmatic types an unpleasant prelude to a reasonable career was to me an introduction to the horror of war.

And so, when we marched through the woods in the rain and our boots slopped through great pools of water and mud and there were, mysteriously, hundreds of dead frogs bloated and bobbing belly up like pale balloons, their tiny webbed hands limp as a flag on a windless day, I felt the sense of it and carried it with me, so that when later drill sergeants shot live ammo above our heads I didn't object.

•

He said I could go to basic training at Ft. Jackson in South Carolina. My recruiter, SGT D, was a large man who covered his face with his hands when he got flustered or found something silly. I liked him. He told me it was called "Relaxin' Jackson," and up came the hands.

We sat across from each other in the small front room of the Ogden, Utah, Army recruitment office. Tan carpet. Tan chairs. Large "Army of One" posters on the wall displaying fit men and women engaged in various feats of heroism. But I wasn't joining the Army to relax. I wanted to take the curtain down and get a feel for the grit of life. When I told him so, he said, *Okay, we'll send you to Ft. Leonard Wood.*

What had really happened is that late one summer afternoon, while I was watching TV and eating sweet cereal in a lethargic trance, an Army recruitment commercial came on. Somewhere in my head, thumping around under many pillowy layers of sleeping in and eating too much and not wanting to commit to anything for more than a week, lurked an intuition, a memory really, that life was about more than running from pain into the comfy arms of self-indulgence. So, when the commercial came on, I put down my Froot Loop–filled spoon and stared as a man ran solo through the desert, his dog tags clanging rhythmically. *He* was not comfy. *He* was not eating snacks until he fell into a midafternoon stupor. He was suffering. It was a choice he'd made. There seemed something rare and pure in the set of his face.

Some months after that first meeting with SGT D, I met him back at the recruiters' office. There were three of us. Three eager kids who clambered into SGT D's black, government-owned SUV. We were headed to the Salt Lake MEPS for a physical examination, the ASVAB, and the DLAB. We chatted excitedly with each other about our ambitions. *I want to be the first woman to be a Green Beret,* I said haughtily. A wispy boy wanted to be an infantry soldier. An athletic, blonde Mormon said medic. We all spoke with such zeal and false knowing about what would come next. None of us knew.

It turned out that I tested into language school—though I didn't yet know what language. I swore an oath there, too. Once we got to basic training, there would be no turning back, SGT D said. We'd go to jail if we went AWOL. We were government property now, he explained, as though it were as natural to become property at eighteen as to pick a college major. That was August 2001, when the sun rained down its photons through thin mountain air and the box elder, white pine, and juniper rattled a dry complaint against a cloudless sky. A month before the September 11 attacks. A month before the Army would be roused, like a great beast, from its peacetime nap.

•

I was still in my jammies when the phone rang. My mom's voice shook. *Get down here*, she said. *The Pentagon's been attacked.* So my brother and I tumbled into the car, and I drove to the university where she worked, and together we watched on her office TV as a second plane crashed into a second tower. Smoke is what I remember. Smoke against a blue sky. I remember feeling that the sky wasn't dressed appropriately. Where were gray clouds? Where thunder? The world watched in horror, and people fell like leaves. They were so tiny.

Later that day I ran two miles along Harrison Boulevard to the recruiter's office. Panting, I strode in and asked if they needed me. *Is there going to be a war?* They were kind as they sent me home. *Not yet, kid.*

•

*You'll be a sheep among wolves*, he said. We stood in the entryway of Transfiguration Greek Orthodox Church. Father Dan had come to the United States from Romania to study theology at Princeton. But many years earlier, in the '60s, he'd been compelled to serve in the Romanian Army under the RPR, the Romanian People's Republic. From what I gathered, it had been a brutal experience. *You are only a baby Christian. Do not expose yourself to such things until you are more mature*, he said. There were few things I wanted more than to please Father Dan, but on this point he was clearly confused. He didn't know how tough I was or how different the American Army was from Communist Romania. His service had been forced. I was going voluntarily, happily. I also suspected a remnant of sexism, though he had not supplied me with any direct evidence of bias. *He probably thinks I'm fragile because I'm a woman*, I thought. I imagined patting him on the head. *Silly old priest.*

A year or so earlier he'd given a lecture on church history at Weber State University in Ogden, Utah. My parents attended and, deeply moved by something he'd said—who knows what—began attending occasional services at the tiny, gray-domed church nestled in the heart of Mormon country. A fine silk of snow covered the roof the first time I went with my dad. I could see the orange glow of candles inside, while behind the church the Wasatch Mountains loomed, running a jagged, north–south spine of rock and snow and wind.

I was seventeen then and just coming off a real losing streak. I had started drinking and smoking menthol Marlboros my sophomore year of high school. Contrary to convention, my drug and alcohol use had nothing to do with peer pressure. If anything, my peers pressured me in the other direction.

Mostly I drank by myself, stealing nips of my dad's Jim Beam and bumming cigarettes from older kids hanging around the coffee shop near our house. Sometimes I went to raves by myself and bought ecstasy and pretended I knew people until the MDMA kicked in, and then suddenly I did know everyone. At parties, people asked who I knew. I would mumble something and walk into another room.

Eventually I did make a few friends. Sometimes a cute boy I liked would let me smoke weed with him. And there was an older girl, an artist, who drove too fast down canyon roads and liked to skinny dip and took me to a secret hot spring.

Sitting there in bikinis, smoking cigarettes in the bubbling, sulfuric water, I learned a lot about men. As she spoke, she paused often for effect and leaned against the rocks, and all that nicotine and ethanol swam in my head until I was lifted straight out of the cumbersome and lonely life I thought had been my destiny.

But then I stole my parents' Subaru in broad daylight to go smoke weed at the cute boy's farm and got the undercarriage stuck on a stump, and the police came and handcuffed me. I was only in juvie for a few days. *Joyriding*, they said. My mom brought me sandwiches on the second day. Once, a guard told me that I didn't belong there. Who knows what he meant, but it got me thinking. We all wore the same tan uniform and walked around in the same cheap slippers. None of us had makeup or curling irons. What could set us apart? But I *was* out of place among the harder girls who came from harder lives and had been compelled to make harder choices. I was just an angry kid who could have just as easily been on a soccer team and going to movies with her friends.

Nothing changed after they let me out. I snuck out at night and slept until noon and skipped school. At a party one night a couple boys undid my pants while I was unconscious. I woke up covered in blood. Wind whistled through the middle of me after that—a wind I eventually got used to and named and carried around like a pet.

Later, my parents kicked me out of the house, so I moved into a friend's basement. Soon, I got a job working a cash register at a bakery in the rough part of town after school. Meth addicts wandered in and out of the store, while I sat in the back eating éclairs. With the little money I made, I bought cans of beans and loaves of cheap bread and brought home trays of stale donuts and lived off that in my friend's basement until my dad wrote me a letter saying I could come home. They loved me, he said, but I couldn't live with them while I drank and used drugs. And I couldn't swear at them. Later I learned my dad wept while writing the letter, and then he walked the four miles to my friend's house and put it in the mailbox.

Why *wasn't* I playing soccer and studying for history tests and singing in the choir? I've asked myself the question hundreds of times. I spent years trying to recall some evidence of abuse, a dark, traumatizing secret that would explain the disease in me. But the truth is, I was raised by people who loved me and fed me and kept me from danger. Turns out, I was just born with a rabid hunger. There's a line you hear a lot in recovery meetings that fit me during those years and for many after: *I had a God-sized hole in the middle of me, and I kept trying to fill it with all kinds of things that weren't God.*

•

By the time I walked into the little Greek church, I'd quit drinking—at least for the moment. I'd done a wilderness program out in Colorado and came back full of life. No booze. No drugs. I worked hard at school for the first time in years. And then my for-all-intents-and-purposes-agnostic parents started going to a weird little church. And then, for reasons I'll only ever be able to guess at, I went, too. And that's when I met Father Dan.

What I remember is a small church. The walls were adorned with icons flecked with gold that danced in the candlelight. Those saints looked in at us from the walls and, I would later learn, loved us and prayed with us. But the first time I went to vespers and for many months afterward, I felt that I was in the presence of something I didn't understand. Not only was the language occasionally Greek, but the movements of the liturgy were foreign to me. We stood and knelt and kissed icons and hands and sang at unfamiliar intervals. The music, too, though it was sung by a few elderly women and only occasionally by a voice student at the university, was beautiful. The sound of it was—though new—somehow known to me. It was the sound of my hunger. It was a wail in minor tones. No victory march here. Just pleading: *Lord have mercy, Lord have mercy, Lord have mercy*. That earnest cry was what I hadn't heard in church as a kid. This church knew about pain. And because it knew about pain, it knew about joy.

There were no contemporary theatrics. No youth programs or welcome committee, but soon after I arrived, I knew I would stay. Think what you may, but when I knelt there, confusedly, a freckled girl in a church full of olive-skinned people, the Holy Spirit lit a fire right where the wind had once blown, and he filled me with himself. And I knew him and loved him and wept.

I sometimes wish I'd heard Father Dan's warning that December morning, a year after I first attended his church, two months before I would leave for Missouri. But I know now only a different kind of girl could have understood what he was saying then. I was too bull-headed. The same girl who invited herself to parties because she wanted to get high now wanted to be a soldier. She'd read *For Whom the Bell Tolls*. She'd read Marcus Aurelius's *Meditations*. She knew about the stoic stance of a man who does what is necessary.

•

My mom likes to tell the story as though she were an oracle passing her hand over scattered bones and sheep guts. February. Valentine's Day, so early it was still dark. SGT D parked on the street and waited in his black SUV. I left the house with a small bag of possessions. I remember the photo of my family. I remember a prayer book. The Army, I'd been told, would supply me with clothing, glasses, toiletries.

My mom, dad, and brother stood in the driveway. I don't remember this part, but my mom says my hugs were hurried. After eighteen years at home, I walked down the sloped driveway, threw my bag in the trunk, and climbed into that black truck on that black morning. I was headed to Ft. Leonard Wood. My family stood huddled in the cold, waving as SGT D pulled away from the curb. With a mixture of pride and sorrow, my mom describes the profile view of my face, how my eyes set on the road ahead and did not turn back.

•

Home was not a word that meant much to me before I left for basic training. It certainly didn't conjure up a sense of a geographical place. When people asked me where I was from, I never knew what to say. *All over* was the answer I gave most often.

My parents met in Seattle. Mom was Dad's student at University of Washington, though she half-heartedly claims they didn't date until she'd graduated. They married in 1980 in a little church on the Oregon coast. She was twenty-three then, he forty-three. A few years later, Dad was teaching at the University of Oregon in Eugene. That's where I was born. Dad tied a pink balloon to the banister of their apartment balcony.

I wasn't Dad's first child. He'd had a son with Esther—another marriage, another life. Greg was about my mom's age, a prodigy, a real, live genius, who worked at CERN after college and had started a dazzling career in small-particle physics. Who knows what he thought of his father's new wife. In the pictures, he is young and handsome and smiling as he holds his new baby sister, all fat and fluffed out in pink ruffles.

Dad taught European intellectual history, the history of ideas. According to Mom, the crib and baby swing hardly fit in the apartment for all the piles of books. Darwin and Hobbes and Plato, Voegelin, Girard, Kierkegaard, Solzhenitsyn. Dad was always about to write something important. I think he'd thought it would happen someday, just after the next thing got taken care of, and the next.

Soon after I was born, they headed back to Seattle, and then on to Notre Dame in Indiana, where my little brother was born. By the time I graduated from high school, we'd lived in seven states and nine houses. I'd changed schools twelve times.

If I thought of it at all, home seemed to me a place I'd never been. The sort of thing a person could spend a whole life looking for. If my parents had been more religious I might have thought of our transient lifestyle in terms of Christian exile. Our uprootedness might have taken on a spiritual dimension. But as it was, our family grew into the habit of lifting our skirts out of the mud of our current state to chase down green fields in the next. We were always headed toward something better: a new job, a better school, a more interesting landscape, or so it seemed to me then. Mom says it was necessity that drove us.

The constant state of flux gave me opportunities to reinvent myself. Before starting at a new school in the third grade, I remember practicing Cool Katie moves in the mirror. At this school, I would have friends, I assured myself as I practiced the posture of someone self-assured and aloof.

It never worked. Wherever you go, there you are—wise words I unfortunately wouldn't hear for another couple decades.

Before the Army, I was forward tilted, putting all my hope on what would happen next. Then I left home. The dark neighborhood snaking away from SGT D's truck in the rearview. And then, far from the familiar smells and habits of my family, I was alone.

•

Every night during basic training, I took out my little red prayer book and climbed up to my top bunk and prayed before falling into a dead sleep. I'd left without my priest's blessing, and yet when the drill sergeants dragged us out of bed in the morning and had us doing push-ups in the rain and sleet, I looked up and saw the Lord fixing the sky with wounds, lightning and purple bruising clouds. And it was beautiful to me. He knew about pain. He knew about joy.

•

It was early April when Alpha Company loaded up into repurposed school buses that rumbled through the Missouri forest. The bus driver played music on the radio—Outcast, Dido, Nelly. It felt strange to hear it. Other than the brief hymns played during church services and the rolling, call-and-answer cadence we sang when we marched, I hadn't heard music in about two months. It felt taboo, a former life coming in through the speakers.

Two months in basic training is not like two months of backpacking or two months of travel or any other adventuresome, challenging thing a person might do for that length of time. Those two months put a seal on our lives. The world we were being initiated into was to be a final world, a world in which and for which we were willing to die. And so the musiclessness of it rattled forward in time and into our bones, so much so that we sat on those torn bus seats listening to the radio in a kind of rapture of transgressive delight.

This day had been pitched to us by our drill sergeants as an extravagant prize. We did not know where we were going, only that we were being rewarded somehow. Some marker of achievement had been met, though I was half sure it didn't exist. The bus ride seemed inevitable and orchestrated. After so much deprivation, here was a reprieve, a caesura, a bright spot that would, by way of contrast, intensify any subsequent deprivation. And so we arrived at a strange, white church in the middle of the woods.

We unloaded from the buses and formed up into platoons and squads, still unsure what to expect. The drill sergeants instructed us to be grateful and well-mannered. *Yes, Drill Sergeant!* we must have shouted back.

Once inside the church, we filed into wooden pews. The church had high, white ceilings. There were columns off to the sides and civilians standing by the columns in pale clothes. The company commander got up and announced that the good people of the church had given their time and resources to support the troops. After a short service, we would all be invited to have a home-cooked meal of turkey and green beans and mashed potatoes. Then we could do what we wanted for two hours: play basketball, sleep, talk—all unheard-of privileges. There would be phones we could use to call home if we wanted. We just had to sit through the service and then the reward would come.

Soon, a preacher stood in front of us and began to talk about Jesus. And just as soon my skin began to crawl. The drill sergeants prowled around the pews looking for heavy eyelids. And I remembered how, just a few weeks earlier, a boy had been discovered sleeping in a folding chair during a lecture on Army Values and how the drill sergeant screeched and spat and then made him do push-ups in the back of the room until we heard a blood-curdling scream. *My heart!* came the panicked voice. *My heart has a hole!* None of us knew what happened to him after that, only we didn't see him again.

The preacher made a clear case: Jesus loved us so much that he was willing to suffer death on the cross. He was willing to suffer a punishment meant for us. And because he did that, we owe him a debt of gratitude. So clean. So easy.

After that, there were hymns. I chanced a look at a friend. She rolled her eyes.

Then the preacher with pressed pants and neatly combed hair offered that if anything had moved us that day, there were volunteers available to guide us all the way to salvation. The people standing by the columns waved. When the time came, Nina and I agreed to see how they meant to get us there. We found a petite young woman with clear-seeming eyes and went with her into a small, white room. She sat on one side of a little table, we on the other. The girl had two small pieces of paper in front of her, one for each of us.

She seemed nervous. I told her that I was already a Christian, baptized in infancy and chrismated in the Greek Orthodox Church. She didn't know about any of that, she said, and looked at me insistently.

*Would you like to be saved?*

*Emphatically, yes*, I replied.

*Wonderful!* She perked up.

*Do you believe that Jesus is the Son of God?*

*Yes.*

She put a little check next to a box. *Do you believe that he came to save sinners?*

*Yes*, I said again.

Another small check.

*And do you believe in the authority of Scripture?*

*Yes* again.

Check. She shifted in her chair. She was more focused now, as though a finish line were in sight.

*And do you accept Jesus Christ as your personal Lord and Savior?*

*Absolutely*, I said.

A final check.

Then she asked me to pray, and I did. Every word in good faith. At the end she handed me a slip of paper. On it was the date and a stamp marking the moment of my salvation. My friend went next.

Then there was food and the wonderful sense that I could stand or sit anywhere I liked. I could stare at the sky if I wanted, and no one would yell at me. There was grass I could walk on. I think it was meant to feel like heaven.

Some boys started a game of basketball, and I watched them laughing and shouldering one another. But my heart was set on home.

I scarfed down the warm meal and headed to a back room, where the church had set up a bank of phones. But there was a long line of kids already backed up into the hallway. Looking at a wall clock, I supposed I'd get a chance if each of them took only five minutes to talk. I squatted against the wall to wait.

I kept a small picture of my family taped to the inside of my locker back on post. It was one of the few personal items we were allowed. In it, all four of us stood under a tree. It was autumn. The leaves were yellow and orange. My mother was beautiful. My father dutiful. My brother looked impish and annoying. And I was very clearly uncomfortable. Family.

Now that I couldn't see them, my heart, which had previously felt only disdain for their many, glaring inadequacies, flipped—just as when someone dies and the stories about them change and it seems petty to remember any shortcomings. In any case, the feeling was so intense that at night I cried. For love, I think. They were the only place I'd known it.

With just a few short minutes left before we had to get back to the buses, my turn came. With shaking hands I lifted the receiver. I heard my parents' phone ring and ring and then the answering machine.

On the way out, I stuffed my cargo pockets with a few bags of Skittles. The whole bus ride back, I hunched over and secretly shoveled little beads of sugar into my mouth until the drug put its numbing glaze on me.

•

In the years since, I've wondered about the legality of the whole thing. It seems unlikely that the federal government would approve sending Muslims and atheists to a mandatory church service. But what bothers me most, I suppose, is the thought of that young woman approaching her pastor with a small piece of paper, upon which, I imagine, she'd written the number of people she'd led through redemption's gate. Were they keeping score? I think of the women who prepped the turkey for us, the paper plates and lemonade. That plain, white church and canned green beans and all those people busy claiming soldiers for Jesus.

I tried to picture a nineteen-year-old kid listening to mortar fire falling all around him. Would he fish in his pocket for the little slip of paper? Would the date and stamp speak into the intensity and violence of that moment? I had my doubts. But what did I know? Salvation is a living and unpredictable thing.

•

We had to qualify only on an M16 rifle, though we learned to shoot plenty of other weapons, too: M9 handgun, M246 machine gun, AT4.

To qualify, we lay on our bellies and propped up our weapon on sandbags. Plastic, green men popped up and down at fifty yards, one hundred yards, three hundred yards. They told us to inhale and then exhale and hold our breath while we squeezed the trigger. It was bitter cold, and I couldn't feel my fingertips through my gloves. Inhale, exhale, squeeze. A satisfying "bing" sounded when a bullet hit a man and he fell backward.

Inhale. Exhale. Squeeze. Bing.

Each weapon carried twenty rounds in a magazine. Twenty bullets. Twenty people knocked backward. Bing. I worried about accidentally shooting someone, or someone shooting me. Like a lot of kids on that range, I'd never held that kind of life-ending power in my hands before.

But I'd read Hemingway, and I wanted to be the kind of person who could do her part. Like Anselmo, I hated the idea of war but wanted to serve something higher than my preferences. So when it was my turn, I lowered myself to the ground and lay my weapon on the sandbags and waited for the enemy to appear from behind little dirt mounds down range and slowly pressed my numb fingertip against the trigger at the bottom of my breath.

# 3

# Anchorage, Alaska

*When the lambs is lost in the mountain, he said. They is cry. Sometime come the mother. Sometime the wolf.*

Cormac McCarthy, *Blood Meridian*

I once wrote a poem about an early memory I have of finding a rabbit in a frozen pond. He was lying on his side, black eye open, little tufts of fur stirred by the wind. The lower half was encased in ice. I stood looking at that rabbit for a long time, wondering if he died before or after the ice got him. Wondering whether it mattered.

We lived on a sloped, dead-end street lined with duplex housing for Alaska Pacific University faculty. My dad was a provost there. I remember liking to remind the other kids on the street that my dad was their dads' boss.

In the winter, the dark became a narrowing vise around our days. With just an hour or two of daylight left, we'd run home from the school-bus stop and grab our sleds and race to the snow-covered hill at the bottom of the street. It plummeted down at a sharp angle into the woods below—the woods with crisscrossed paths and moose and rabbits, dead things and living, where small, beautiful sled dogs raced on the first day of the Iditarod.

We took our green and red and yellow plastic sleds and shot down the back of the hill and ran back up it until we steamed. And sometimes we'd stop and visit the old, abandoned ski hut, where cross-country skiers used to build fires to warm up on long trips. But no skier had been there in years, and we said that it was haunted and climbed onto its roof and fought each other with sticks.

Once, when we were playing by the haunted hut, and the dark was creeping in and purpling the glossy snow, one of the older kids suddenly let out a shrill, blood-curdling cry and ran away. The other kids ran, too. But I was on the roof, and it took me a second to get down, and by that time everyone had vanished. It was then I felt the black fear. Something evil, just behind, almost touching me. My vision tunneled as I ran, so slowly it seemed, down the trail, a right turn, then the hill.

When I got to the top, the other kids were laughing. A joke. But my face was white, I'm sure. All of us knew that those woods were not just any woods. Or, they were. But they were not safe. Death could be played at and had.

•

When my parents told us we were moving to Alaska, I thought of igloos and polar bears. In fact, when my dad flew up there to interview, I warned him repeatedly about the bears. *Don't get eaten, Dad.*

I was six and thrilled, apart from leaving my best friend behind in Kentucky. When we finally arrived I was only slightly disappointed to learn that we would not be living in an actual igloo. Tall, white birch trees stood in straight-backed clusters, their paper bark peeling off in sheets. And fir and pine. Red-capped mushrooms dotted the yards that ran like an unbroken field the whole length of our street. Our new home was a dark, green duplex at the bottom of the street, the last house before the dead end and the hill and the woods.

We lived in the top half. There was a mudroom for boots and coats, then a tiny kitchen, dining room, living room, and two bedrooms. I didn't think it was small then. It was perfect. We had a brick chimney for climbing, and bunk beds. And there was a hideout in the bathroom, a deep cupboard cut high into the wall. By standing on the toilet paper dispenser, we could launch ourselves in and shut the door—a world apart from the world.

•

Some people say that the land can make a person, that if you live somewhere where the wind blows and the sky is open and the sun layers its heat over the earth in equal doses, those realities rear the soul, giving it some piece of themselves.

If it's true, then some part of my soul is made of birch and dark and snow. And another is made of so much light a person can hardly sleep. A soul of extremities. Anchorage is a normal-sized city plunked down in the middle of a vast, humanless wood. There is, among the residents, a sense of rugged awe over the persistence of humankind and an even greater awe over the powers that aren't ours. It's a way of thinking that's hard to re-create in, say, San Francisco or Detroit.

From time to time, Dad would take us out into the wild. He'd been a part of a mountaineering group in Seattle and had caught the outdoorsman bug. Before they were wed, my dad somehow talked his very indoorsy fiancée into backpacking the Olympic Range with him. In a photo, my mom is smiling, but later she would tell me how much she'd disliked it. How her ill-fitting boots gave her horrible blisters. She'd felt inept and tired but had wanted to please him.

It was lucky for his children that Dad didn't take feelings into account. Lucky that he insisted, despite our protestations, that we come with him to the mucky banks of cold rivers on rainy days to fish for king salmon. And lucky he packed his five- and eight-year-old children into his green Mercury van on the weekend to climb mountains or go for long hikes. Many Sundays after church, we drove down Highway 1, where the road traces the Turnagain Arm, a crook offshoot of the Cook Inlet, to Alyeska, a little ski resort in Girdwood. Out the window, we'd see eagles and dark fir and icy water lapping at mudflats. "Mud flaps," we'd called them, as we studied the innocuous-seeming stretches of mud with a sense of horror and reverence.

On the way, Dad loved to tell us stories about tourists doing stupid things and dying from it. One of our favorite stories, a story that filled us with a sick sense of fascination and dread, was about a newly married couple. The way my dad told it, they were not Alaskans. We knew that because of what happened next. The bride, still wearing her wedding dress and a large fur coat, walked out onto the mudflats to have her picture taken.

The impulse is understandable. The Kenai Mountains tower off in the distance—the stark, inhuman beauty of them rising into the sky above the ice-slate waters. It is wild country. A perfect backdrop. In any case, she walked out onto the mudflats without knowing that they are basically quicksand. Who knows how long it took for them to realize the problem. Did her husband take pictures first? Was she smiling? In the end, he watched his new wife slowly sink into the mud. And there was nothing anyone could do.

I used to try to think of ways she could have been saved. A giant straw to keep her breathing until they could think of something better. (My dad pointed out that there was almost no way to keep the straw in her mouth.) A helicopter could have pulled her out? (It would have ripped her in half.) Why didn't they amputate her legs?

Alaska was full of stories like that.

•

I did not love being outdoors in the beginning. What I liked was eating soup out of a bread bowl in the ski lodge. I liked that my dad gave me a few Snickers bars to keep in my ski-coat pocket in case I got hungry on the slopes. "Good energy," he said of most candy bars. On hikes, I liked the trail mix and the occasional cookie.

But skiing itself was terrifying. I used to stand at the top of steep slopes and imagine the many ways I could die going down. I worked myself into paralysis, and on several occasions I ended up taking off my skis to slide down on my butt.

My brother, who started skiing three years earlier than I, at the age of three, felt as natural on icy gradient as I did walking down a sidewalk. He did not so much ski as plummet. Once, he sailed right off the edge of a ravine and was spared injury or death only by the saving arms of a few scrappy trees that had grown from the side of a cliff.

So my father was caught between us: my athletic brother flying heedless toward possible disaster and me, a slightly plump, anxious girl frozen by fear at the summit. Often as not Dad could be found waiting somewhat patiently at the bottom of any given run, yelling at Henry to wait and then imploring me to find something like courage or sanity enough to make a first, slow turn.

But I was busy wrestling with death up there. From where I stood, it was clear enough that if I were to edge my skis downward, I would lose control. And if I were to lose control, I would almost certainly be decapitated by a tree.

Most of the time, I did coax my skis toward the slope and did allow gravity to do its work and did manage to avoid the trees, and when I fell, it was often in soft powder. And because, year after year, my dad kept bringing me, despite my being a large pain in the ass, I encountered fear and learned to ride it.

On the way home from Alyeska, Dad gave us Jolt energy drinks and more candy bars, and he played the Eagles and the Kingston Trio, and we sang as loudly as we could and barely noticed the mudflats out the window. And when we got home he handed us—wired and exhausted—back to our mom and took a nap.

•

Soon after we moved to Anchorage, I started first grade at Lake Otis Elementary. Then, in the middle of second grade, my parents transferred me to Northern Lights. In third grade, I went to Saint Elizabeth Ann Seaton, a Catholic school. And in fifth grade I returned to Lake Otis. A great, dysfunctional circle.

I think they were looking for a good school. A better fit. I'm not sure now. What I remember was the feeling of being a perpetual newcomer.

My mom had a kind of religious conviction about my genius. She put my art on the walls not because she thought it was cute but because she thought I was brilliant. I'm not sure any of the schools I went to quite agreed with her. Maybe that was part of the problem. I also wasn't good at normal school things, like homework or paying attention or keeping papers in a binder or getting my parents to sign permission slips. Most days, I showed up late, dreamily thinking about—who knows what—as I wandered into the classroom, unaware that I was interrupting anything.

Once my fourth-grade teacher, Mrs. Evans, called me up to the front of the room and had me walk back and forth in front of everyone to demonstrate my slow gait. She was angry with me a lot. I was slow about most things, only ever half there.

Part of the problem might have been that I was supposed to wear glasses. They'd been prescribed in the third grade, but I knew they would hurt me socially. So I left them at home and instead very coolly stumbled around the world and squint-glared at everyone. In one parent-teacher conference, Mrs. Evans brought up the fact that I made mean faces at her all day long. I don't think any of us realized what she was talking about until I was well into my twenties.

Eventually, I was referred to a school psychologist for testing. My mom wanted me in classes for the ultrabright; my teachers wanted me in special ed. It was a confusing time. After a barrage of testing, the results came back confirming both teachers and mother: the kid is smart when focused but astoundingly inept at all other times. A few years later the diagnosis would have been ADHD inattentive type. But thank God no one thought of it then. I escaped Ritalin and instead persisted in being a flamboyantly awkward, ill-managed kid.

Back at home, Mom persevered in her convictions. She enrolled us in piano and art classes. We were not allowed to watch TV or eat ordinary kids' snacks like Fruit by the Foot. Instead, we ate rice cakes with peanut butter and orange juice smoothies made with raw eggs.

At night she read us chapter books: *The Lion, The Witch, and the Wardrobe*; *The Black Cauldron*; *A Wrinkle in Time*.

I curled around the left side of her body to read the pages along with her. My brother, who perched on the arm of the couch and was always backlit by lamplight, could not read, a fact I relished as though it were (and it was) a final, fleeting sign of my superiority. In those evening trances, there was perfect harmony and love among us. We bent over the pages, each of us attuned to the cadence of a world we did not inhabit. A world we somehow longed to enter. There was the smell of Mom and the feel of her cool skin, and her throat became a channel for the lives characters lived elsewhere, over there.

•

In the second grade, I twisted my foot inward and hobbled up to the teacher's desk complaining that my leg hurt. She was not amused, she said. But I didn't want to amuse her. I wanted to go home.

More specifically, I wanted to lie down somewhere cool and dark and just look at the texture of shadows on a wall for a long time. I was tired of trying to keep up. Tired, too, of the constant, grating sense that I didn't belong. I fantasized about being home with my mom. She would have to take the day off work if I were really hurt. She would sit by me and we could talk and maybe she would stroke my hair.

Between the second and fourth grades I claimed illness or injury almost every day of school. By the time I reached fifth grade I'd grown a little savvier, but the impulse was still there. And so very early I developed a habit of lying.

I also started living with a new kind of moral tension within myself. I knew I was lying, and I knew that the teachers knew I was lying. I could see the disdain on their faces every time I claimed a fever or eye pain or swollen lymph nodes. But I couldn't stop. The need to get away from there was so overwhelming that I was willing to look foolish. In a childish way, I accepted the penalty of shame in the hope of somehow escaping the school day.

And maybe in a way I *was* sick. An ill-formed child. An ugly child who insisted on herself. A detached and dreamy and confused child. But what kind of medicine could heal a problem like that?

•

In the summer, when the days were long and school was out, I'd ride my bike over to APU's main campus to explore. Sometimes I stole money from my mom's purse to buy candy from a vending machine. Sometimes I went into the student commons and looked pathetic until someone got me an ice cream cone. Sometimes I'd sneak into the theater building. The back door was rarely locked. Backstage, in dark and echo, I ran my fingers over green, feathered masks, swords, empty flasks, a sheepskin.

It was all a little illicit, I knew. I was behind the curtain. A kid, no less. A kid people rarely wanted around. But the theater was a portal, the kind I'd come to look for everywhere. Velvet curtains and wigs and a table littered with fake food—all of it suggested to me that adults also wanted access to something more. They wanted to cross over. A part of me, maybe the larger part of me, believed it was possible.

And so, when I left the theater and walked the wooded path behind it and found iron lampposts along the way and painted stone animals and living toadstools, I felt that I was getting closer somehow—that tilted and bright realm just out of reach.

•

On Sundays we went to church. It was an Alaskan Lutheran church, which is to say Scandinavian. The services themselves conjured up feelings of discomfort. Itchy clothes, platitudes, my parents acting polite, an expectation that we would do the same. That high-up-there cross draped in crafty fabrics had nothing to say about the dark wood or dead rabbits or my own wild hunger.

I do not know what I thought of God then, or if I thought of him at all. He wasn't mentioned much at home, apart from rushed dinner grace. I do not think I prayed in those days. The thought of it was itchy.

But in the winter, we went to church camp. And there we ran in the snow and went sledding and ate sweet cereal for breakfast. Counselors advised us not to wear bright hats because owls were known to swoop down with immense claws to lift scalps from skulls.

In this churched forest, there were dangers I knew and dangers I didn't. And, when it grew dark, and we huddled around a fire and sang along with Pastor Fritz's melancholy guitar, there was something else, too, that moved in the dark. Something that felt animate and strange and personal.

•

The summer after psychological testing, my mom left my dad. We were walking up our street, I think headed to a dinner event on campus. It must have been summer because we weren't wearing coats. Halfway up the road, my mom told us that she would be moving into an apartment.

I ran home and shook with rage. The whole world could be turned to dust. And now it was. She had done it.

At night I had nightmares about my mom entangled in darkness. In one, she sat next to it, the darkness, on a park bench, and I flew toward it and clawed its eyes, as though it had eyes. But in the daylight we quickly grew accustomed to the new order. Sometimes we were with Mom. Sometimes she played Michael Jackson and danced in the strange, new living room. She gave us candy and tried to make it fun. And sometimes we were with Dad, who cried (the first time I'd seen it) as he pulled the garage door shut, and who told me between quiet sobs that he loved my mother very much.

•

I started stealing more. I stole twenties from my mom and gave them away to kids on the street. I stole small toys and candy from stores.

Sometimes I got caught, and then my mom or dad would make me go back into the store and tell the manager what I'd done and give it all back.

Sometimes, I hid in the pantry and ate whipped cream from the can.

Sometimes, I ran down the dark street with the stars overhead and the cold wind thrashing my face. I imagined myself a wolf—unencumbered by human thought, wild, wordless, howling.

•

At eight years old I was incapable of imagining what might have passed between my parents. Theirs was a private world that only sometimes exploded into the yellow light of our kitchen—Mom hurling a coffee cup or whacking Dad with a newspaper.

What the kids saw, what we saw, was Mom's volatility and Dad's long-suffering. How unfair children can be. Because Mom was a good parent, she didn't make her case to us. It came out in accidental comments decades later, little snippets that over time began to paint a new picture. Dad the husband: controlling, superior, aloof. Once, just after we'd moved to Indiana, and Mom was six months pregnant with Henry, and I was three, and it was the hot end of summer and the new house didn't have AC, Dad took off for Seattle. To get the old house ready to sell, he'd said. For three months, he hung out by himself and visited friends and ate at restaurants and drank beer in the afternoons and, yes, painted the house. All the while his wife was mowing the lawn in one-hundred-degree heat, her belly getting in the way of the lawn mower handle, her rambunctious daughter yelling for popsicles or crying over a cracked and empty robin's egg.

And there was the time even earlier in Eugene, just after I was born, that Dad went on unemployment to write a book while Mom worked and tried to breastfeed me and sometimes took me to work with her and then put me in daycare. But Dad didn't write. He sat among his books, his typewriter silent. *I'll have something to write after I read Darwin's letters or once I read so-and-so's commentary on the letters or once I read the other so-and-so's critique of the commentary,* I imagine him thinking.

His filing cabinets and his library expanded, and my mother bent to the work required of her, and I went to a crappy little daycare, and my mother grieved it, and we never knew why she threw the coffee cup at his head.

Shame must have piled up. He'd been meant for greatness, or so the story goes. Dad's intellectual achievements would justify all the sacrifices others had made for him. The wife he left because she couldn't keep up with his advancing career. The years of grandiosity and bourbon and women. Later, his pretty, new wife bringing home the bacon six months after having a baby, so he could get it done. Finally. And every day that went by without writing, he might have, must have, felt as a reproach. And shame drove him away from Mom, the unconscious image of his failure. And so, she left him.

But all we knew then was our pain and Mom's decision to inflict it.

•

It was difficult for me to make friends. Once, a few days into a new school year at a new school, I decided the thing to do was pretend to be sad. So, at recess I sat on woodchips near the swing set and cried into my knees. Two girls approached me to see what the matter was. Naturally I told them to leave me alone. I was mourning a breakup, I claimed. When they offered to console me, I grew angry and stormed off. I'm not sure, in retrospect, what the strategy was there. Sadness + anger = pity = pursuit = friendship? Maybe. But I didn't get to the pursuit part. Instead, I was understandably relegated to the outer edge of the social system. I and a few other kids orbited out there. Sometimes we made a play to jump toward an inner circle, especially if one of us had become a special object of scorn recently. We'd use that leverage to thrust ourselves closer to the normal kids. But it never lasted. We were weird, and out we fell again.

There was a girl with short hair. She'd had chemo, she claimed.

The kids called her a rat. There was a slightly manic and ill-dressed boy with whom I agreed to write space stories. There was a gangly boy with a large forehead. When he came over, we pretended to be spies and crept around my neighborhood peering through windows and sometimes threw moose turds at people.

•

I don't remember when my mom moved back in. She wasn't gone long. But it was long enough to hurt us. She came back with her bags full of things that had once seemed an immovable part of our home, as she had been. And, like a broken piece of ceramic, she made a scraping sound as she slid back into place. My parents were careful around one another in those days. Later, I learned they went to therapy. Later, I learned about my mom's remorse and the intensity of her grief.

But at the time it seemed to me that the universe had crumpled around her weakness—a weakness I came to associate with all women and loathe in myself. It didn't happen all at once. I was only a child. But my feet started sliding over toward my father's side of the aisle. I craved order and a steady hand, his slow voice and apparent fortitude.

If it had not been for my mother's leaving, I might have continued down the innocuous-enough-seeming road of willful otherness—the rebellion of the nerds, etc. But she did leave, and so I gravitated instead toward the fantasy of male impassiveness. Years later it was that fantasy and the further thought that I could harness my father's strength, become it, that drove me from teenage indolence into a brutal, masculine world. I went into the Army to strip the female from the male in me, mystery from reason, poetry from prose, weakness from strength.

Luckily for me, it was not to be.

# 4

# Monterey, California

*Sappho begins with a sweet apple and ends in infinite hunger.*

Anne Carson, *Eros the Bittersweet*

He told us we were the cream of the crop. We were standing outside the barracks in our BDUs learning how to treat abdominal injuries and apply torniquets. There were soldiers lying in the grass pretending to have been hit by a mortar, and we bent over them and pretended to place their guts gently on their shirts. Afterward, a staff sergeant told us how special we were. Linguists, he said, were the best the Army had to offer. He was, of course, himself a linguist.

I'd arrived in Monterey right after basic training. If you've read Steinbeck, then you know the scene. The windswept cypress perched on a rock thrust out into the breaking sea. The sea-rot stench of sea lions clapping and honking in a morning fog that sits fat and unhurried until the sun is high. The scent of salt and tin.

But Cannery Row, Steinbeck would be surprised to see, is no longer a place to work and then drink to forget the work. No longer "chipped pavement and weedy lots and junk heaps, sardine canneries of corrugated iron, honky tonks, restaurants and whore houses, and little crowded groceries, and laboratories and flophouses." Now, there is an aquarium and expensive gift shops with blown glass and little twirling kites out the window. High-end restaurants and atmospheric bars. The whores don't paint their faces anymore. Aren't even paid anymore. And the "gamblers and sons of bitches" wear golf shoes and tourist hats and military brass.

But rich sin is not really so different from poor sin, only maybe less uncomfortable. And so the world when Steinbeck wrote was still the world in 2002, when I arrived in spring, the gulls swooping at trash cans, and the light folding in soft layers on faces and sand. That spring the ocean sent its salt coat way up the hill and dropped it onto the high terra-cotta roofs and treetops surrounding the barracks where we lived.

The Defense Language Institute sat high above the rest of Monterey, high on the city's domed and dead-grass peak. The institute consisted of a small city of buildings: living quarters organized by military branch and schools organized by language. I would eventually land in Foxtrot Company, a row of clay-colored barracks at the summit of it all. So high and green up there—bishop pines and cedar and sweet-smelling sky all around.

The light salt air made things seem possible again. The ocean was wide. Still, each morning we fell in line. And there were drills. And after language school, we ran as a unit down the hill and into town and through it. The locals knew us by our stupid PT uniforms and the way we used crossing guards and reflective belts even in broad daylight. Sometimes we ran on the beach and sometimes past shops. And I felt our otherness as I flew past wealthy bohemian tourists and kids playing in the sand, normal people living normal lives. We were about something else, our awkward galloping seemed to say. Our black and gray clothes made us almost indistinguishable from one another, a line of sweating youth getting ready for the war.

•

When we arrived in Monterey, we were first put up in a small, white building until our language classes started. In the white building we were all Army soldiers, but we were headed for different schools.

Some to Chinese, some to Korean, some to Russian, or Thai, or Farsi, or Arabic. Category 5 languages (Chinese, Korean, and Arabic) took the longest to learn. Category 1 languages (Spanish and French), the shortest. Each of us was assigned a language based on a test we took when we signed up. I was glad I hadn't tested higher. I'd hoped for Russian, and Russian was what I tested into. I would be in Monterey for a year. A few days to learn the Cyrillic alphabet, then lists of vocabulary words, then the accusative case, genitive, prepositional, the accent and idioms. *Gde toofli?* I'd ask after three weeks. *Tam na polu.*

In the white building I made friends with a soft girl. Brown hair, brown eyes. Rounded at the elbows and chin. She was smart—soon she'd start Arabic. She would have eighteen months to learn, then she'd be sent . . . who knew where. We weren't at war yet, but we knew what was coming. In my room we'd pull out little tablets that had our new alphabets printed on them, and we'd practice. I loved to hear her command the sounds, already foreign to me. Right to left.

One day she whispered to me that she was going to camp overnight with a boy she liked. It wasn't allowed—not yet. No overnight passes until we got to our more permanent unit. She asked me to cover for her, and I agreed. She borrowed my sleeping bag. *Do you need a tent?* I'd asked. She laughed. No, she said. She wanted to see the stars.

I understood her giddiness. The night sky, cypress black against it, the sharp wild scent of the ocean, the thought of the Monterey Canyon deep under water, all that mystery just there, you could point to it. And then walking on grass, and no one to yell at her for it. Then running on it. Naked. The boy and her, running that way in the dark.

But the next day she came back and would not speak except to tell me to wash my sleeping bag because it had poison oak on it. When I went to her room, she was holding a lighter to her skin. Burn marks all up and down her arms. *It's the only thing that makes it feel better,* she said, and pointed to the pattern of pink pustules running over her skin, up her face, her stomach.

Her eyes were empty in a way I knew, and maybe she saw it in me, too, because she began to cry and told me how she had changed her mind, and how he pushed her down in the poison oak. And after, he got in his car and drove away.

And so she burned her skin, and for days she burned it. And it was a relief.

•

Class started two weeks after I arrived. Of course, our teachers were Russian, meaning they loved their language, meaning they were from the very beginning disgusted with us for not knowing it. The women especially were sharp and demanding and exasperated by all of us, except Solnishka, a beautiful, blond Airman who learned languages the way the rest of us drink water. He opened his mouth, and the words poured in. The Russians smiled when he spoke.

There was a Ukrainian woman who told us that she loved Kiev, and she clutched her chest as she said, *from the midst of my being*. And a large Polish man who would enter the classroom breathing heavily and then plop into a chair and begin telling us stories about the Soviet Union—smuggling cigarettes and jeans, hunger, the men who drank jet fuel when the booze ran out. There was a young Russian woman who tsk-ed over the girls, advising us to eat only every other day, and who wore white pants and dark thongs. She was brilliant and beautiful and hard to understand, but the boys hung from her bottom lip.

That's how the days were spent. Listening, speech, grammar, vocabulary, history. Repeat. Then, in the warm afternoon, just when sleep was about to curl over our eyelids and put them down, class would finish, and we'd change into black and gray PTs and do flutter kicks and push-ups in the dry grass and run sprints and call cadence to remind us that we were not in any normal kind of school.

•

Before barracks inspection, I popped a few Stackers and pushed play on my CD player. Snow Pony. A synthetic, manic sadness filled the room. Just right. And I buzzed around looking for tiny specks of dust and wrinkles in my shirts and socks turned sideways in their drawer.

Ephedra was new to me, and I loved it. I bought the weight-loss pills in gas stations and grocery stores. I liked the thought of them twitching me toward thinness. I wanted self-control, and ephedra seemed to give it to me. I had little appetite and lots of energy for work. But more than that, it let me take about three steps back from life. Those little yellow-and-black pills protected me by making me indifferent. So what if Gospozha Tatyana scowled at me as I stumbled around inside the instrumental case? I was far away, humming behind my face.

Some years later, the drug was taken off the market. I can't remember why except there was a story about a woman who caused a terrible accident. She claimed psychosis—that somehow the weight-loss drug had driven her mad, and so she wasn't responsible for the acceleration or the turn or the inability to care for the lives just two hundred yards ahead, then ten yards, then no yards. She was not herself, she claimed over and over again.

I knew it wasn't safe. I took the pills at prescribed times. Never before a run—I'd tried it once and my heart felt lumpy and dysregulated halfway through so that I'd had to stop and walk back. Instead I used it to focus on boring things like cleaning and vocab. And sometimes I took it before class. And sometimes on weekends when I wanted a little lift and a little barricade. It was nice.

•

There is a saint in the Orthodox Church whom I love and think about often. Saint Mary of Egypt is said to have lived in the fifth century, though the dates are uncertain. When she was twelve, she ran away from home to Alexandria, where she became a prostitute—not because she needed the money (she often refused payment) but because she was driven by passion, which is another word for addiction, which in her case meant nymphomania.

When she was nearly thirty, she joined a ship of pilgrims traveling to Jerusalem. They were going to see the true cross, a fragment of which was housed in the Church of the Holy Sepulcher. But she was not interested in the cross. Along the way, she seduced as many men as she could away from the path.

I think of the famous icon of the Ladder of Divine Ascent that lives in a monastery at the foot of Mount Siani. In it, men and women climb a dark ladder that ascends into a gold-flake sky. But there are skinny, black-winged creatures pulling the climbers over into an abyss—of what? It's not clear. But Saint Mary of Egypt is figured doubly—both climber and demon, falling and pulling others down with her by the pant leg.

She's not the sort of person you normally picture with a halo. But there she is, in Orthodox churches around the world, hair matted, bones showing, eyes burning.

God came for her. He'd probably been after her the whole time, but he doesn't seem to ever force a person into loving him. For whatever reason, he caught her at the door of a church. She wanted to go in with the other pilgrims but was kept from entering by an invisible force. I imagine her outside the church, looking in. And then—this is the miracle—she wept.

Afterward, she made her confession at a nearby monastery and received the Eucharist for the first time and then crossed the Jordan out into the Wadi Rum desert. She had three loaves of bread when she left. Once that was gone, she lived off whatever she found in the desert—locusts, snakes, the occasional egg? For forty years she starved and was alone.

That's what repentance looks like, I thought. What wouldn't I do to taste the mercy of God? Such an idea in the mind of a twenty-year-old girl is a dangerous thing—holy and unholy hungers sitting so close together the boundaries lose their meaning.

•

The girl picked up an egg and took a bite out of its white head. Into the bowl made by her bite, she dropped a pool of Tabasco and took another bite. Again a red pool, now mixed with yolk. When she looked up, she saw me watching her and grinned. *I'm trying to drop a few pounds*, she said. *I'm going to try out for the Army run team.* Lean in her uniform, the fabric folding in to meet her fine ribs and whisper legs, she finished the egg. Her plate was empty.

We were in the chow hall. Around us hundreds of soldiers hunched over bowls of cereal and bagels and omelets in the din. Loud voices bounded from wall to wall in the minutes before a bell would chime, and we would all leave for class. I looked down at my plate, which minutes earlier had held buttered toast and scrambled eggs and cantaloupe. It had seemed a reasonable breakfast to me, but I was suddenly embarrassed. The girl told me she had run cross-country for Duke before joining the Army to pay off student loans. She was a Chinese linguist. So smart. So fatless. So (this part I didn't form with language so much as intuited) utterly beyond reproach, which is to say *powerful*.

As she stood and walked away, I studied her form again and made a decision. It did not occur to me that the girl might have been inwardly tortured by a need to excel, or that later that night she might have had a burger and painfully rebuked herself. What I saw was a path out of the near-crippling sense of myself as under the world's heel.

The next morning I put a hardboiled egg on my plate. Then I sat and picked up the egg and took a bite out of its head, and into the little bowl made by my bite, I poured a small pool of Tabasco. The heat made the egg seem more than itself.

But by 10:30 a.m. my stomach was growling. During a break between classes, I snuck over to a vending machine and bought a granola bar and sat on a curb in the sun away from everyone else eating it and hating myself for eating it.

At lunchtime, I realized I didn't know what to eat, so I had an orange and tuna with no bread and ate the fluffy white of the orange down to the peel. But again I grew hungry.

After school, I put on my PTs and joined my platoon for training. In the heat, I felt faint and did not run as well as I used to. I did not fly. But there was a kind of victory in that too—the knowledge of a secret battle. No one else knew how hungry I was, how impressive my speed, given the circumstances.

The next day I tried again. No granola bar this time, I told myself. I felt lightheaded in class and couldn't recall the vocab I'd memorized the day before. The next day, I raided my roommate's snacks while she was out, Oreos and yogurt, vowing to replace what I took. But of course she noticed and was annoyed, and I was ashamed. And ashamed, I went to the grocery and bought her food, more than I had taken.

And so a war began. Restriction, hunger, purity, indulgence, shame. I knew that if I could get the technique down, I would conquer the uncontrollable hunger in me. But the more ashamed I felt, the more puritanical my restrictions became, and the more frenzied my binges.

I began running long distances to get rid of my mistakes, as though a person could do that. Ten miles. Fifteen. On sand and through town. I signed up for the Big Sur marathon and began to justify my running and restriction that way, as though athletic excellence were the goal and not the means.

And so the rule was established. Moral purity became conflated with hunger and sin with eating. As the god of my interior world, I dealt out punishment when it was deserved. I ran to repent of cake and cheese and peanut butter. I ran to reassert my goodness. I thought it was up to me, like that.

•

Some Sundays I met up with an Air Force girl studying Farsi and a young Serbian woman who taught in the Serbo-Croatian department, and I would drive us to a little Greek Orthodox church south of Monterey. We chatted about Dostoyevsky and Orthodoxy and Colin

Powell's recent UN testimony on weapons of mass destruction in Iraq. Lena, the Serbian, said she thought *The Brothers Karamazov* was too dark. *He is so gloomy. There is a sickness in his mind*, she complained. She spoke with the languid authority of a European woman. I felt her accent somehow trumped my affection for the novel. *But Alyosha?* I'd offered weakly. *And Staretz Zosima?* She waved her hand. *He thinks too much of men. We are cripples. I have not met a man with dignity*, she said, and she began to tell me about Serbia—the war, the cruelty of her mother, how genocide is not a word that means anything. Genocide. There was only meanness and rubble and violence that was sometimes very close and sometimes far away. *And once you see that, you do not read The Brothers Karamazov. You want to read something happy instead.*

Outside the windows the Salinas Valley whipped by. Fields of cabbages and then forest and hills. And pale, salted light, the dust of it everywhere.

Marina, the Farsi linguist, sat silently in back. She was the daughter of a priest and very practical about her faith. I think she might have been practical about everything she did. At least outwardly, she didn't seem to wrestle with goodness. Maybe that's what humility looks like, I thought, watching her face in the rearview mirror—how she gazed out the window, taking the poppies in.

We were almost always late. Lena was unbothered, but Marina seemed a little flustered. I'd get caught up in conversation with Lena and miss the exit. This did not happen one time, or two, or three, but nearly every Sunday. At some point, Lena started offering to drive.

Since leaving Utah, I'd longed for church. In the mornings and evenings I often pulled out my little red prayer book and said the prayers. I wanted back what I'd had. The slaking of thirst. The presence of that intimate holiness. But this new church in Salinas was not like the old church. I felt none of the same fire. It was like starting all over again. I stood in a pew next to beautiful Lena and practical Marina and crossed myself self-consciously, waiting for God, I thought.

# 5

# Ogden, Utah

> *No synonym for God is so perfect as Beauty. Whether as seen carving the lines of the mountains with glaciers, or gathering matter into stars, or planning the movements of water, or gardening—still all is Beauty!*
>
> John Muir, *John of the Mountains*

The summer before I started eighth grade, we moved to Utah, just forty minutes north of Salt Lake City. The air was thin there, and light did not glisten and spread so much as it thwacked a person across the face. Light with nothing in its way. A dry and cloudless sky.

That summer, I was fitted for contacts for the first time and left behind the old glasses/squint-face paradigm. I was also allowed to shop at the mall for school clothes. No more Land's End catalogues or Fred Meyer discount clothes. Dad took me, and I probably visibly shook with anxiety as we walked into Zumi's. I kept thinking that one of the clerks might come up and gently suggest I try Ross Dress for Less. But no one did. I ran my hands over boardshorts and skate shoes and looked longingly at the belly shirts only thin girls could wear. Eventually, I picked out a couple of baggy T-shirts and a pair of cargo pants.

But when I turned to find my dad, he wasn't there. *Dad?* I called out, intensely embarrassed. *DAD?* I poked my head out of the store to see if he was reading on a bench. No dad. It was then that

I saw my father's feet sticking out from under a rack of coats. His head and torso were hidden. I bent over and shook his shoe. From inside the dark cave of fabric, I heard a grumble and a sigh. He'd been napping.

I know that I turned red because that is the color associated with the temperature inside my head. Dad slowly pushed the coats aside and got to his feet. At the cash register, I dumped the clothes on the counter and looked at the floor while my dad fished out his wallet. Walking back to the car, I looked at my dad with a weird and uncomfortable mixture of embarrassment and admiration. Who could care so little about what others think?

•

I was probably wearing those very clothes when I met the cello that fall. The details are foggy, but I remember walking into the gray orchestra room for the first time. A few of the kids had clearly been playing since kindergarten. One pulled out his violin and, with great seriousness, ran his fingers through a little dance on the black fingerboard.

Soon, the teacher walked in. His white button-down strained against his belly, and his pale underchin wobbled as he gently instructed those of us who had no instrument to pick one out. We wandered among the wooden bodies trying to imagine which voice would suit us best. I settled on the cello. I liked her depth. The open G sounded like shipwreck, gravity, sorrow—stuff I was into.

The cello followed me home on the bus and then back to school, back and forth like that all year. At home, I practiced for hours, compelled by the hope that I could wrestle beauty out of that long throat. There was a startling intimacy between the cello's hollow body—her silver cords, curve, and pins—and my own body. Her voice, it seemed to me, was my own, and I sang it out between my knees. Something in the very middle of me, something like obsession or awe, started vibrating. I was lost inside the wooden box.

My parents were thrilled. It seemed I had found something good at last. The swamp of self-pity aired out as I put my hands through the drills, up and down the fingerboard and side-to-side the bow, commanding the whole house with the sound of my private love.

Soon, my bow screeched less, then not at all. Within months I started private lessons with a music teacher at the local college. And then my instructor said he thought we should start preparing for Interlochen. Devotion like mine was uncommon, he murmured again and again. There are two kinds of cellists, he told me, mathematicians and artists, people who play for technical precision and those who play from a well inside themselves. I was the latter. But, he reassured me, I could acquire technique.

I felt a red cord inside me pair and sing with the music of chafing bow and taut string, of hollow and low. A long, deep note buzzing the skull and teeth and eye sockets. And my body swayed in its chair in tempo with the music. Boccherini, Lully, Bréval, Bach.

•

I'm not sure that we were conscious at first of wanting to please my dad. Henry now claims that his prodigious sense of humor emerged entirely from a desire to see my dad chuckle. I think if I had been beautiful, I would have seen his delight in me and wouldn't have had to try so hard to win him over. But what a blessing I wasn't. He raised me like a boy and, I think, thought of me that way. And so I wanted to please him the way a boy pleases his father. I mirrored his work. I asked him to teach me. I wanted to be brave and competent. A good driver. A solid citizen.

But I wasn't naturally any of those things. I was cowardly and inward and loud and insecure. Plus, Dad was remote. He didn't want to talk about Plato with thirteen-year-olds. He didn't want to have us in his most important world—his intellectual world. And so Henry and I each settled for finding a collection of ploys that would get an approving grunt or handshake or, best of all, a laugh.

Henry tried baseball and motorcycle riding and, eventually, he cracked the philosophy door. He was granted entry to the inner sanctum.

Meanwhile, I was able to occasionally solicit approving nods by running and hiking and speaking in short, unadorned, observational sentences. When I helped him in the backyard, he sometimes patted my back and offered me orange-flavored soda water. But he did not want to talk to me about books. I was too wild a thinker for him, untethered to the house of learning he had built. Years later, when any male professor thought I wrote or read well, it was a shock. And a shock to my Dad, too, when I earned high scores in tough classes—but all that came later.

It's not that Dad was cruel or unloving. I now know that he loved us both deeply and probably never noticed the two of us running around behind him, nipping at his coattails. It just didn't register with him, for instance, that when his daughter approached him with outstretched arms, the natural response would be to hug. He would raise his hands in defense. *Stand back,* he seemed unwittingly to say.

•

I started high school in 1998 at Ogden High, a castle of a school that had been built from brick and plaster and asbestos some sixty years earlier. It was not a rich school. Half its students came from below the train tracks, half above. Which meant half were poor. Half had cars to drive after they got their licenses. Half needed free lunch. Half wore Tommy Hilfiger. Half wore Walmart specials and hand-me-downs.

That freshman year, I took a class in Shakespearean theater. Our teacher coached us through the plays, line by line, explaining the surprisingly relatable emotional intensities of *A Midsummer Night's Dream* and *Hamlet*. I loved it. We read lines aloud and acted out scenes until the dead language sprouted little green shoots of life.

Before, the words had meant almost nothing, little bodies inert on the page. But under our gaze, they rose.

Suddenly, I was not just a kid running my hand over props but a slightly older kid striding across an echoing black stage, light on me, my own throat a channel for a kind of beauty and complexity I did not know how to express on my own. I could step into the life of Puck or Rosalind or Lady Macbeth and their voices could live in me and I in them, a kind of borrowed resurrection.

•

I don't remember my first drink. I don't even remember the first time I got high. I'm not sure I liked any of it at first. But persistence pays off, as my dad used to say. And so I kept drinking—I think mostly because I had a new crush.

He had dark hair. Dark eyes against pale skin. His older brother was a semisuccessful drug dealer in town, or at least that was my impression. His family was poor. They had a little spot of land outside of town where they kept horses and Doberman pinschers. Their house was always dirty, always smelled vaguely of manure and hay and something sour. But the boy liked having me around, and so he gave me weed and booze, and it all felt a little like God probably meant the world to be. *Fear not*, Jesus had said. An impossible command unless you had a little vodka in your belly or half a bowl of smoke in your head. How easy and bearable the world seemed to me, how lit up. I felt I could love and be loved at last.

Of course, the adults in my life were against it. They didn't understand the expansive horizons I'd been introduced to. They didn't know it was all about God—much more so than their anemic pieties on Sunday, or so it seemed to me. I came home high. I let them know about it. Flaunted it. Felt the power of my position in their helpless anger, the look on my mother's face after she told me I was grounded and I walked out the door. What could they do? What would they do?

•

It didn't happen all at once. But maybe it seemed that way to my parents. One day, I was playing the cello, the next I came home with blue hair. The next I said *fuck you* to my dad. Then I ran away from home. Soon, I threw a big, very lame party at our house while my parents were out of town. They found me the next morning hungover, carrying giant trash bags of cans and bottles to the trash cans by the curb—to hide them presumably, but it's not clear that I had an actual plan. I lied and told them I wasn't sure why the house smelled like cigarette smoke. Why the trash bags. Why the dog was still drunk. Why I was. I shrugged and tried to look innocent as a red Solo cup popped free of the trash bag and rolled down the driveway.

My already weak grades plummeted that year. I dropped the cello midway through the second trimester. Then I was cast as a witch in *Macbeth* but found it difficult to get to rehearsals. Teachers expressed concern to my parents. I drank at school, brazenly, in the hallways.

Around that time, I introduced my little brother to weed. He was twelve. I'm sure I thought I was doing him a favor. I wanted him to see the world I'd found. A world underneath the world we lived in—where life exceeded itself, was bright and glorious and unmitigated by the tedium and discord of sobriety.

Just a couple blocks from our house, there was a golf course, and beyond the golf course rose the humped backs of the Wasatch foothills, and out of those rolling hills towered the sharp-angled spears of mountain I came to identify with something exhilarating and free—something I could not quite name but wanted to. Henry and I walked through the golf course and settled underneath an orange-leafed oak. I pulled out my stupid apple bong and made him take a hit. He coughed and was terrified, and then we walked home.

Later, I took him to a rave. The bouncers didn't let him in, so he waited in the barely lit parking lot outside while I went in to buy ecstasy from a stranger. Two hours later, when I came out, Henry was angry and hurt. I didn't think much of it then. It annoyed me that he was making a fuss, and I regretted bringing him along. In any case, I didn't take the pills that night. Instead I put them in a little bottle full of No-Doze and forgot about them.

A few weeks later, in the middle of a morning English class, my heart started racing. I'd taken No-Doze that morning. Or thought I had, but I hadn't really looked at the pills. Was I rolling? Did I buy bad ecstasy? Was I going to die? I grabbed my backpack and ran home. Down in my bedroom, I shook the pills onto the carpet and saw two bluish, stamped hexagons. It was fine. I was fine. My heart was the normal heart of a teenager who stayed up until 2 a.m. and ate No-Doze like candy. Some hours later, Dad found me playing computer games in the basement. He was wearing a bathrobe. He might have asked why I wasn't in school. I might have given a made-up answer. But he went back upstairs, and I turned back to *Baldur's Gate*.

•

After I left for the Army, Henry got messed up with a kid who did coke. A sweet kid whose parents didn't like to be home and who gave him money instead of themselves. The boys watched gangster movies, and one night when the dealer didn't have coke, they bought meth. Henry totaled Dad's Ford Explorer while coming down from a three-day high. He'd taken Ambien and fallen asleep at the wheel and ran into a snowbank. Our parents sent Henry to rehab. Then Mom took a job in Juneau, and they moved. And even though there was coke and meth in Juneau, little high-schooler Henry got sober at eighteen.

His friend didn't. He ended up breaking into an old lady's home, tying her up, and robbing her at gunpoint. In an article in the local paper, the elderly victim was quoted as having emphasized the boy's kindness. He was a polite boy, she said, even while he was tying her up.

Years later, Henry reminded me of the day with the apple under a mountain oak, the smoke that filled his innocent lungs. He said I was not responsible for all that came after. Still, I think of the contagion I spread. Not that I made any of it attractive, but that I left a hole where goodness might have been. Instead of a loving sister, he had an elder sibling who was utterly preoccupied with herself, her freedom, the drama of rebellion, the flight from herself. I showed him the tunnel I was digging. Out. Sin of omission. Sin of commission.

•

That was the year of running away and getting kicked out. The year of juvie and community service at an old folks' home. The year of loss. The party, the boys, the blood. I had fallen in love with beauty so quickly. And just as quickly, my strange, mostly solitary rebellion ended those loves. Instead of practicing the cello or memorizing monologues, I found myself hitching rides to raves no one invited me to.

I had given up on proving myself to Dad. He could have his stuffy expectations and secret life. Instead of pleading with him to embrace me, I told him to fuck off and stole his car in broad sunlight.

But none of it was quite as bold as I imagined then. I would have given anything for a hug. And maybe anger was my incoherent way of saying so. Dad, in his too-short shorts, a Nalgene bottle filled with vodka and Gatorade in one hand as he mowed. The Mormon neighbors looking on. Yes, that strange man. When I told him I hated him, what I meant was, *Drop the Nalgene and chase me across the lawn and we'll laugh again*. I meant, *Help*. And, *You're losing me. I'm losing you.*

•

In a last-ditch effort to pull me back from the brink, my parents sent me on an Outward Bound course. I remember sitting on our blue-and-gold-striped sofa when Mom handed me a pamphlet. Mountaineering, it said. There were pictures of kids my age belaying from sheer rock walls and trekking through high alpine meadows. Why I agreed, I cannot now recall. Maybe I hoped I would acquire a sexy, outdoor bod for junior year. Or maybe I really liked the idea of the adventure. Or maybe I saw my parents reaching out in love.

In any case, I agreed, and in June, Dad drove me to Durango, Colorado. I could tell he was proud of me. He seemed lighter, happier than he had in months, and he kept patting my arm as he drove, as if to say, *You'll be all right, kid*. We stayed the night at a Best Western in Durango, and the next morning I boarded a bus with twenty or so other kids—all troubled by drugs or anxiety or fat or some other ailment our parents hoped to fix. We were headed for the back country. Twenty-one days in the wild.

I was not in shape when I arrived. I remember standing in a meadow before we headed out that first day. All our gear was spread around us, and the instructors kept telling us to put more and more things into our packs. Sleeping bag and mat, water bottles, clothes, tarp, gaiters, rain jacket, first-aid kit, food. By the end, our packs weighed about forty pounds each. That first day, we hiked carrying our packs over rocks and the foothills of mountains.

I trailed behind the group most days, demoralized and sorry for myself. But then there were clear mountain streams and high, grassy hills that made me feel that I could run them straight off into the sky. Purple flowers shining in morning dew, the sun just about to crack the horizon.

One morning, it was my turn to make breakfast, so I sat outside the tarps (we didn't have tents) heating water over a propane fire. It was still dark and quiet in that high meadow. And then, alone in the silence of morning, I prayed—despite my relatively recent rejection of Christianity.

When I opened my eyes, God answered my prayer with beauty, somehow shaking the quiet valley below so that I could see it better, see it had been made to be seen—soft petal leaves and the curving shapes of hill and saddle and, above, violent rock broken off at the sky. I prayed without knowing what I needed, only, I asked for help. I expected nothing, but that day as the sun bore down on us and we were driven over mountain peaks, I felt wings on the heels of my hiking boots. I had never felt lighter. It was no effort at all to lead the group at a breakneck pace all day and then to drop my pack in the grass and race up and down the rocky hills that towered in a half circle around our camp. It was in my body, this joy. And it wasn't mine. That's all I knew.

•

Love came first. It had to be that way. No one was going to convince me of anything about God. I'd already decided that Christianity was a bedtime story adults told themselves because they didn't want to look reality in the face.

I say love came first, but something must have preceded even that. God's hounds after me, nipping at my heels, gently pulling my shirt by their eyeteeth. Only, I wasn't aware of any of that. It just occurred to me one day that instead of saying *fuck you* to my parents I would ask if I could join them at church. It seemed like my idea, then. I'd sniffed something new in my parents' speech—gentleness or solidity—and I wanted to see what it was all about.

And then I was there in the darkish sanctuary. And then, what can I say except the old words? I fell. The world opened to me, light covering it. The planets had been made by the same God who moved blood through my veins. I fell off my high steed, hitting the ground in dust and blinding light.

In those early months, God pounded my heart with joy. It was like a grass fire out west on the eastern side of the mountains, whole fields razed and made rich by a storm of heat. I burned down. Wounded by love, abandoned to it, flung out, and I didn't care how strange it made me. This God, the animating power, the face of Christ serene and insistent, had caught me in a net, and it felt like freedom. It was, I think, the only real freedom I had ever known.

In the years to come, my mind would circle back and back to those months, that fire of proximity. Time would never march forward again for me. Now life moved away from or toward that center, as though someone had caught the fabric of my life by a clothespin and hung it from a branch.

•

I came back from Outward Bound a different kind of girl, in some ways. The wilderness had taught me a little about the relationship between pain and beauty, between sweat and joy. And so, when I left the sun-whipped trees and mountain peaks and Colorado monsoons and returned to the temperature-controlled indoors, I tried to retain the lesson.

But it was a mixed effort. I didn't know yet the real nature of my problem. Back at home, I mostly stopped drinking and ran long miles in our neighborhood and up into the Wasatch Mountains. But it wasn't enough.

That year, my dad let me sit in on one of the classes he taught part-time at the local university. They were reading Marcus Aurelius's *Meditations*. Dad bought me a copy. He was letting me in at last, I thought.

What I found inside that book was everything that was missing. Order. Virtue. The hope that I could become an entirely different kind of person.

I also found what I thought was my father. The rigor he demanded, his confidence in reason and moderation—his desire to retreat from the excesses of his children, their loud, flamboyant, unbridled passions. My actual father never did talk much to me about the book, but it didn't matter. Because I could talk to Marcus. He was a map to my father's heart, and I read him and marked his thoughts until the pages were worn and ink-smudged.

•

Father Dan chrysmated me in November 2001. Three months before I left for basic training. One year after stepping foot in an Orthodox church for the first time.

During the year leading up to chrismation, I attended almost every service. Not just liturgy on Sunday but also vespers and weekday feasts. And every Tuesday Father Dan taught a class for catechumens. The liturgical life of the Orthodox Church was unlike anything I'd experienced before—not in Lutheran churches or Catholic or Baptist. The *sense* of holiness, the presence of it, wasn't something I had to imagine. And so, when I learned that the Orthodox believe liturgy is the actual meeting of heaven and earth, that the church was, in fact, the mystical body of Christ, I knew it was true. The presence of God became so much more than an idea, became a living reality I could (and did) experience. God up close, known and experienced, but also essentially mysterious.

During liturgy the priest prayed that God would make him worthy to celebrate the holy mysteries. He sang about the six-winged and many-eyed seraphim, soaring aloft on their wings. There were deep prostrations. And right alongside all that formality was organic human movement—how natural it was to see people walk around the room, bringing noisy children to icons or lighting candles, standing or bowing or crossing themselves. The sharp musk of incense, its body the body of our prayer somehow rising.

I wouldn't have said it this way then, but what I experienced was the end of metaphor, or the fulfillment of it—the tenor plunked down in the middle of the vehicle. The body was the bread was the body. Symbols ceased to point away and instead became the thing they represented. The icon of a saint was an actual living face. *Just think of kissing someone through a window*, Father Dan had said. Tempera and gold leaf, eye and halo.

•

There seemed to me a wonderful overlap between Orthodoxy and Marcus's stoicism. I had learned from Father Dan about the desert fathers. Their teachings on sin were unlike anything I had heard in Sunday school growing up. Sin, it turned out, was not a crime in the normal, judicial sense. Sin wasn't about rule breaking; it was about illness. The goal was to be a person fully alive, the glory of God (as Saint Irenaeus put it), but on my own I was full of sickness, cowed, hair falling out.

But that was not all. It turned out that the action of sin was only a part of the problem. The desert authors of the eight deadly thoughts (which would later morph into the seven deadly sins) claimed that the whole battle took place in the mind, long before any death-dealing act took place. That's Marcus. The things you think about determine the quality of your soul.

All of them seemed to be saying in one way or another that I could and should set my will against myself. The higher part at war with the lower. Reason against animal desire. Strength against weakness. I fell in love with the idea of winning out against the disease in me. Stoicism offered the (unfortunately quite un-Christian) thought that I could set my will against hunger and subdue it. Of course, it was a hopeless mission. But I didn't know that then.

I remember asking my dad one day if he thought Christianity and Stoicism were almost the same thing—because to me, they were. The Stoics didn't understand God, but they seemed to understand virtue and how to get it. I remember my dad looking past me as he said, *No, I don't think so*. And then he walked away.

If he had cared to elaborate then, I'm not sure how much sense it would have made to me. Or, maybe he was as confused as I was. Either way, I was headed to the Army soon. And there I would learn how to suffer well. And I would be formed into an unassailable kind of person. The higher part of me would reign over the lower. And Marcus or Christ or my dad, I intuited, would be pleased.

# 6

## Darmstadt, Germany

*There are places like this everywhere,*
*places you enter as a young girl*
*from which you never return.*

Louise Glück, "Averno"

After basic training, after language school, after further job training, I arrived at my first real post in Darmstadt, Germany, setting foot in Europe for the first time. Until then, Germany had been a place I'd only read about in books. Outside the airport, I lifted a large, fallen leaf from the pavement. *A German leaf,* I sighed in wonder.

Back in Utah, I'd looked at SGT D with scorn when he told me he'd been stationed in Germany for two years but couldn't speak a word of German. *Ich möchte ein Bier bitte*, he finally remembered. What a waste, I'd thought.

Darmstadt was a smallish city, just thirty or so minutes south of Frankfurt by train. Frankenstein Castle sat high up on a hill in the Odenwald. Down below, there were plenty of little restaurants and an art museum that had an exhibit of crude Picasso sketches. There was a train station that seemed made entirely out of steel and glass. And on the outskirts of town, strawberry fields and dairy farms. Much later I would learn that during the reign of the Nazi Party, Darmstadt was the first German town to force Jews to close their shops.

Of course, the city was unlike any American city I'd encountered. Stone paths were hundreds of years old, and many buildings boasted similar longevity. There was a sense that something quite old was leaking up from the earth, up through the soles of my shoes and into my blood, as though history were animate and hungry. Sometimes I walked around like that, with a sense of time's depth and power, and I'm sure my mouth hung open sometimes even when there were no monuments to gape at—just the plain sense of death's formidable march, and life's countermarch.

Darmstadt was bombed in World War II, which I think adds to the kaleidoscopic effect of time's imprint. Unlike Rome, where history absolutely dominates, an oppressive thunderhead of time, Darmstadt was rebuilt and modernized. Only some of the old structures survived, and they stood in sharp contrast to modern Germany: sleek, minimal, chrome, blue-lit.

During in-processing, we took a week of German from a local instructor. She was funny and bright, and we quickly became friends. Anna introduced me to döners and the idea that water should always bubble. And she took me shopping. In the H&M underwear department, she explained that thongs were far sexier and more comfortable than "granny panties"—the underwear I had, up until that moment, simply thought of as underwear. While rummaging through bins filled with lace and silk, I mentioned that I was Orthodox. *Ah ha!* She said. *So you know about Princess Elizabeth!* I must have looked confused because she shook her head and began the story of Princess Elizabeth of Hesse, who had been born in Darmstadt.

She was supposedly a great beauty. At twenty she married Grand Duke Sergei Alexandrovich, a member of Russia's royal, tsarist family, and moved to Russia. Born a Lutheran, she soon converted to Russian Orthodoxy and became quite devout. But then in 1905, her husband was assassinated by Bolsheviks. In the months that followed, she sold all her jewelry and rich clothes and founded a monastery for women.

Thirteen years later, after most of the royal family was shot to death in Yekaterinburg, she was taken by force from her monastery. She and a few others were thrown down a deserted mineshaft and left to die. *Here in Darmstadt, there is a memorial garden, a statue*, Anna said.

I chose pink. And as I carried my plastic bag full of sexy underwear out of the store, I thought very briefly about the woman whose body crumpled at the base of a dark hole. And then I did not think of her again for many years.

•

Kelley Barracks was a small outpost just off Eschollbrücker Straße. There was a large, grass parade field in the middle of everything. All the buildings looked down on this field. It's where infantry units gathered with their flags before deploying to Afghanistan. And where our small company formed up in straight rows in the dark predawn for PT.

Sometimes we ran down the street, sometimes out into the woods behind the barracks, out the gate guarded by MPs with M16s and German shepherds, past the yogurt factory that abutted our little post, sending huge, perfumed plumes out of its smokestacks: vanilla and orange.

That fall I lived on the bottom floor of a decrepit barracks building. I shared a room with a girl named Angelique, who had nothing to say to me. She was Military Police and liked to watch *Sex in the City* and eat mini donuts. After spending a year and a half in a training environment, where drill sergeants randomly inspected our rooms for improperly folded socks, I was shocked to see garbage litter the floor. Clumps of hair blew wispily, like tumbleweeds, when the door opened.

Our two sides were separated by a partial wall made of our two movable wardrobes. The unmovable walls were beige-painted concrete. There were many identical rooms on our floor and the floor above and the floor above that.

The girls' bathroom was on the second floor. I learned quickly that all the females, as we were called, showered and then marched through the hallways and downstairs or upstairs to their respective rooms wearing only a robe. And so I bought a pink bathrobe and joined them. And what the males saw or didn't see was none of my business.

•

When I arrived, I was alone. And so, when the boys knocked on our door and offered me Malibu and orange juice, I didn't say no.

They got me drunk and themselves drunk. Once, they brought out a chair and a tall handsome kid, the kind I would have had a crush on in different circumstances, gave me a lap dance in front of everyone. Even drunk, I was uncomfortable. But drunk became the way we all got along. Drunk was what happened on the weekends: stumbling into walls, making out with each other, passing out in the hallway. Whatever innocence I'd arrived with went up like a sweet-smelling cloud.

I kept a journal back then. One of the early Germany entries had a badly drawn picture of a shot glass in front of a mouth. There was an Orthodox cross in the middle of the glass, as though I were drinking the cross, or as though the cross were judging the drink—I'm not sure which. But to the side of the drawing I wrote in a kind of devastated awe of the prison the barracks had become. I couldn't travel, it seemed, because every effort to get away was cut off by someone suggesting I join them at the Irish pub. The prison walls were set by booze and the doubly intoxicating sense that I was a part of something, that I belonged at last.

Sometimes I thought of SGT D and the disdain I'd felt for his failure to learn German, and I offered a silent apology.

•

During the daytime, I was expected to be at the company building. I quickly learned that there wasn't an actual mission for linguists of my sort, so I was given the nonjob of cataloguing the entire library. It was an endless job. It was a job that didn't need doing. All the books were already catalogued. *A new system*, they said. But I'm not sure even they believed in it. Later, I would be asked to rake rocks and pull near-invisible weeds. And later still, once they found a desk for me, I would learn that my job was to look busy. Take endless safety courses, pursue certifications, organize someone's binder.

Booze and boredom. It was not the desert I'd imagined. But futility is its own kind of suffering. And dirty barracks life—that particular claustrophobia that comes from working and sleeping and kissing and exercising and living with a single set of people—gets a person feeling dry.

•

By the time I arrived in Germany, I'd discovered that I was a good runner—faster than most of the boys. And strong, too.

As far as the leadership was concerned, it didn't matter that I didn't have a real job; I was ready for the fight. Fitness means something different to soldiers than to college students. Universities love their athletes, but the kids in the bleachers aren't thinking, *Wow, he's strong enough to pull a wounded body out of the line of fire*. They aren't thinking of the practical, life-saving utility of athletic ability. But that's how it was for us. Athleticism took on a moral bent. A fit person could be a hero, a martyr. The unfit were liabilities. And the shame they endured was unlike normal fat shaming. For us, an overweight person could be deadly—or so the argument went.

A colonel from an adjacent unit started a half-marathon run team. A few of us were recruited, and soon we were racing in Prague and Dublin. I was given new freedoms. I didn't have to do PT with the rest of the unit. I could run when I wanted for as long as I wanted. Sometimes I took off for ten- or twelve-mile runs out into the country or into the city where I found beautiful, old graveyards.

It would be hard to overemphasize the honor of sanctioned independence. Nearly the entirety of our lives was regimented, collective, organizational. We were meant to think that way, breathe that way. And so when I was allowed to train by myself, it was as though I were crowned. Everyone could see me speeding off by myself, away from the pack.

•

I did not stop believing in God during those years, but belief became painful. The contrast between my life and goodness—real, deep goodness—had grown too sharp. Sloppy, intoxicated nights were followed the next morning by grit under the eyelids, hair shirt skin, the faint then sharper memory of dancing, the realization that I was a moron. Or, scenes of near-sex or half sex, hands here or there. All replayed in agonizing, shame-drenched slow motion.

Sometimes, I'd run toward town and stop on a bridge and watch the train tracks curve away into the woods. I didn't know what I was looking at, but something in me reached out to the place where the track bent and I couldn't see any farther. And I wanted to follow.

Then came winter. It was snowing when I took the train up to Frankfurt. There was a Coptic church there, and I wanted to attend the Nativity Vigil. But I got lost in the city and began asking strangers if they spoke either Russian or English. Could they help me find the church? It was dark outside and there were fewer and fewer people to ask. By the time I arrived at the doors of the church, a thought had begun rattling around my head and had grown so noisy that I didn't lift my hand to the door. It had been too hard a journey. Perhaps God didn't want me there. So I turned around and left.

•

It wasn't the same mine shaft, though my pit was also dark and inescapable. I wasn't a saint thrown down. This was something I'd chosen and then chose and chose again. It was a darkness composed of cowardice and self-absorption and alcohol and shame. And the hole was how flung I was out there, twenty and an idiot among other idiots far from home, each weighing himself in the eye of the world, each bewildered and running from something. And out front was the threat of sand and mortar. So we stayed inside the little concertina wire pen and left to pasture at the Irish pub and were all around hemmed in by an unnamable fear.

•

When I walked around town in uniform, Germans looked away. Once, I passed an elderly woman in the street and said, *Guten Morgen!* She spat on me and hurried away. Can I blame her? What had war meant to the Germans? And we Americans were loud and drunk in restaurants and swarmed their cities. Of course, there was also the fact that most Germans opposed our invasions of Iraq and Afghanistan. I imagine they saw us blithely kicking back mojitos and thought of the stupidity of our country, the giant, trampling foot of our international presence.

But that day, it was me, a plain girl who at that moment appeared as a symbol to the woman who spat. And so when she spat, she didn't fling mucus at a person, and I suppose I knew that, which made it worse.

•

The next year, we moved into new barracks. The whole building still smelled like fresh paint and sawdust. Once, a boy I didn't like snuck me into the barracks while they were still under construction. He had a plan, I suppose. But I wasn't drunk enough.

Now, we were unloading our uniforms and boots and TVs and civvies and posters into rooms on the third floor. The floor below us was empty, reserved for an infantry unit that was still serving out a deployment.

The rooms were small, but we didn't care. No mold or stains or decades of rot and dust.

•

I remember a girl who lived down the hall from me and who wore thick eyeliner and was very thin. She talked a lot and her eyes darted around while she talked. She seemed like a glass pane about to crack. Rumors spread that she was bulimic. Some guys started a joke about the boxes of Diet Coke at her desk. I can't remember what I said then, except that I laughed.

We worked in little cubicles, though "work" is a strong word for what we did. We grew listless and apathetic. Sometimes I wrote little poems at my desk. Sometimes I read. Sometimes I fiddled with my computer.

During breaks, I went to the tiny closet gym down the hall and did bench presses and ran on the treadmill in my boots and uniform. Calories in, calories out. Sometimes, for reasons that dwelled far below the level of my conscious understanding, I found myself at the vending machine, my face hot and hands shaking, and I would buy three or four candy bars and secret them over to the bathroom, where I would sit in a stall in the semidark and drink a diet soda and then inhale the candy, barely tasting it. And then, making sure no one was in the bathroom, I would lean over the toilet and let it all up.

Then I would wash my hands and wipe my face and brush my teeth, and a wonderful narcotic calm would come over me, and I went back to my little, gray work pen.

I say calm, but I was numb. And then, a few hours later I would start to feel again. Then I would feel horrified by what I'd done—I didn't understand why I'd done it or how I could stop.

I spent hours in the gym. If I'd been a professional athlete, it would have all made sense. But it was just me whirring and crunching away the feeling of failure—the panicked sense that I might never crack the code or be free again.

The binges got more extreme. Once, at night, I was an addict knocking on barracks room doors, asking if anyone had kids' cereal. It had to be kids' cereal. Fruity Pebbles or Golden Grahams or Cocoa

Puffs. I offered twenty dollars for a box. It was a hit I needed. Childhood, the sweet and forbiddenness of it. And also the numb. I wanted to taste what I couldn't have and then undo it. I wanted to reverse the clock, scramble God's order, have my cake and eat it, too.

Another time, I was at the commissary. I forget what I had in my basket. A family pack of Twizzlers, ice cream, Little Debbie cakes, Fruit by the Foot, maybe. Unhealthy kids' treats my mom never let me have. Then a friend, a good, sane man I respected, saw me. He looked at my basket and maybe the way my hands were shaking and my eyes kept darting around, and he asked if I was okay. When I said yes, he put a gentle hand on my shoulder and asked if I wanted to go for a walk before buying all that food. How did he know? I smiled and probably laughed a little manically and said I was fine.

In years since, I've seen the look on many women's faces in grocery stores and coffee shops. When I worked at Starbucks after college, I thought I could tell who was going to throw up their drink. It was always thin or normal-weight women, often younger. They ordered extravagant drinks, all caramel and whipped cream—something illicit—and were jumpy waiting for it, and the eyes were restless, feathery, and something in them seemed remote.

Men and women who are addicted to food but don't throw up have a different look. They don't float above themselves but are settled deeply, resolutely inside themselves. The drink will go in and be felt and will stay, consequences be damned. Rebellion and acceptance all at once. Middle finger to the world, I want what I want.

•

Imagine how hungry the boys. So new to manhood. For every ten of them, there was maybe one girl. Imagine the Penthouse cutouts in the boys' rooms and taped inside cubicles at work. Imagine the gossip surrounding the girls who took off their pants, the girls who were willing to be touched. Some boys went to prostitutes. Some stayed indoors with their computers. Most of them were at the bar where

I and the other slender collection of girls went to numb whatever needed numbing.

In civilian life, the impulse for men is the same. But in civilian life, there are more women, so all that sexual energy spreads out like butter thinned over toast. But in our tiny barracks world, a fat glop of it sat on each of our heads.

I thought of myself as a virgin then, though of course I wasn't. Somehow my mind had scratched out the implications of what happened in high school. I remembered the party, the gross, older men sitting on couches watching young girls fade. I remember eating mushrooms and the wobbling moon above the lawn. I remember the beer, the vodka cranberry, the soupiness of my limbs, heavy and flopping, as I fell into someone's bed. And all that happened next. But what I told myself then and for years to come was that it didn't count. Actually, I don't think I was even that honest with myself. It was more like my mind was a record that skipped that scene. Or maybe it was more like I knew about the scene, but I could not draw a straight line between it and myself, so I was a virgin.

But by my second year in Germany, I no longer considered myself a virgin. There was no romance, only occasional, horrible mistakes. And the next morning I saw the boys in formation. The boys I barely liked to talk to. And then we worked and ate and partied together and they with everyone I knew. There was no shortage of stories about me or any of the other girls who made the hollowing error.

It wasn't that I'd forgotten the clear teaching of the church on matters of sex and drunkenness. It just seemed to me then that I was not in a place touched by the church. Its holy hand did not lay on our barracks. I was in exile. To survive, I absolutely had to drink, and when I drank my clothes came off. That was it. I was down the mine shaft.

Not all girls got drunk. Some were older and had been around long enough to see through to the other side of drunkenness. There was a pretty girl named Sarah who was Catholic and educated. She was maybe twenty-four, ancient by our standards. She went to church and traveled and laughed and was not, by all appearances, deranged.

There was a good boy named Keith, whose goodness I loved. He and Sarah eventually married and left the Army and had a Catholic number of children and did not, I think, spend any time the way veterans so often do, crawling on their hands and knees.

What I'm trying to say is that not everyone was ruined down by the military the way I was. Some came in with an interior strength I lacked. I'd joined to get it, thinking the Army would build it up in me. But I felt that I was made out of hunger. An illustration of me at the time might have my body small and my mouth immense, the whole world rolling onto my tongue.

But emptiness poured into emptiness sates nothing. I did not pray, though I thought a lot about prayer. I began writing poems, which seemed an adjacent activity, a way of drawing near to something true and putting down its little body of music. And so I wrote about how much I wished God would stop the slow tunneling descent I'd begun. And I wrote bad poems about moral pain, the relative freedom of animals to become what they were made to be. Why, I wondered, was it such a strain for us to be, to become human? Even knowing God, having tasted his light, having bathed in it—I could not will myself to obey him.

•

I forget why we were in the married-housing part of base. Maybe one of the girls was house-sitting. Candace was there. Candace who made me laugh. Candace who mocked people for grammatical errors. Candace who was small-boned and large-haired and Texan. Her boyfriend had proposed a few weeks before, drunk and stammering at a concert. He'd climbed onstage and professed his love. They would be married in a few months.

It was dim in the condo, and soon I was drunk. I remember laughing with Candace and dancing. I remember Candace and her fiancé leaving happily. Much later, one of the couples went back to the master bedroom.

I don't know when I passed out on the couch. But at some point I woke up to someone's glasses glinting above me. His sweaty hands. I drunkenly shoved him off. He fumbled with me, his sweaty body and gross wet mouth. And then he left, and I drifted back into darkness. And when I woke again, another boy was there. One of the boyfriends. And it was the same, only worse. Again, two boys.

•

A few months earlier, a popular, athletic boy broke into a girl's room at night. I remember her name but not his. She reported him, but the unit rallied behind him and whispered about her: *Slut*. Eventually, she was sent off to another unit. I never heard anything about her again. And so it was.

I told Candace about what happened at the party. She asked questions. The boys denied. The girlfriend insisted that nothing had happened. Not her boyfriend, not his best friend. I didn't report it and instead stood next to them at morning formation. And because I'd been asked to train people who couldn't pass the Army fitness test, I had to help one of them. In the gym, I remember kneeling on his toes while he did crunches with a weight. Between reps he'd hand the weight to me, and then I'd hand it back. Fifty like that. And every time his sweating face rose up, his glasses glinting in the fluorescent gym light, I imagined dropping the weight on his head. Glass scattered on the floor.

A few months later, there was a goodbye dinner or birthday—something mandatory—at an Australian restaurant. I was seated across from him and his wife and their two-year-old son. Not a blink of shame. Alligator in my mouth and the kid on his lap.

•

The infantry soldiers came back. They swarmed the floor below us and were pissed when they found that we'd been sleeping on their couches and using their kitchens. But eventually we made peace, and the linguists and the sand-weary kids started drinking together in off hours.

That's how I met Jeremy, a boy who grew up in a trailer park in Georgia and who read Nietzsche and the Russians. After a while he invited me to his barracks room where ten or more tired infantry guys were gathered to read poems. We read poems we wrote and poems we admired. And those big, muscled kids wept. None of us could have said why we needed it, but there was something about getting words down to a prism, memory down to sound and image. There was an urgency in all of us, as if the only way to stay human was to write. They wrote about limbs blown from bodies; I wrote about God. And somehow we knew we were all writing about the same thing.

# 7

# Kailua, Hawaii

*I seem to myself, as in a dream,*
*An accidental guest in this dreadful body.*

Anna Akhmatova

We left Alaska when I was eleven and moved to Hawaii. Dad had lost his APU job and found another at Chaminade, a private Catholic university in Honolulu. We rented a house at the top of a small hill in Kailua, on the lee side of the island. There were coconut trees out front and apple-banana trees in the back. Sometimes after a rain, the heat from the blacktop sizzled the water until it started to rise back up, and I'd walk the road in silence. Thick mist rose up all around my feet and wrapped around my knees, and I could dangle my hands in it as I walked, like a mythic queen.

I started out at Aikahi Elementary, one of the better schools in a state where public education is notoriously poor. And though I hated the unyielding summer and humidity, and though cockroaches and giant centipedes crawled through our home, and though I was a new, very white, very *haole* girl, it all seemed basically tolerable. Though, I missed Alaska's cold and dark and moose and didn't understand a culture built around water.

Soon I made friends with a girl, the daughter of an Army colonel, who lived down the street. Carol had a rare skin disorder that made her skin look like hardened fish scales. I never asked her about it. She didn't seem to want me to. Somehow, I learned that Carol applied an acid cream to her skin twice a day to slough the scales, and there were cracks between the little diamond plates on her face and hands and legs where red lines of blood appeared. Despite the fact that her body seemed to point univocally toward pain, she had a beautiful singing voice—made somehow more beautiful by the contrast—and perfect, white teeth when she smiled.

We fell into a happy preteen existence, talking about boys and walking down to the supermarket to buy cold vending-machine sodas for fifteen cents. We had sleepovers and listened to Boyz II Men and Mariah Carey on the radio, and sometimes we went to movies and all of it felt like it was supposed to—we two girls pining for love, imagining the moment when someone (Tom Cruise of *Top Gun*, perhaps) would see one of us and perceive the beauty hidden away under all the superficial layers our peers were too shallow to look past. And then he would love me (or her) and I (or she) would be lifted up, and the whole world would see what had been invisible but always true: beauty, radiance.

At the end of sixth grade there was a dance. The air was hot and muggy. Bright, wet stars sagged in the sky. Off in the distance, the ocean could be heard licking the sand, curling over it, swallowing it. It was my first dance. I wore a dress that made me feel pretty, and my mom had helped with my short, frizzy hair. I didn't have any friends at school, but somehow I still expected the dance to be a little magical. A prince, a gown, a story about love. But inside the dance hall, where the lights were dim expect for a disco ball glittering up the floor, I was alone. I sat in a chair and watched the other kids dance with their friends and crushes. Sometimes I got up to get punch, but as the night went on I felt more and more a barbed mix of self-pity and resentment. I wanted to cry or yell to make them see how painful it was to be excluded from life.

And then my longtime crush walked up to where I was sitting and asked me to dance. Somehow he'd seen me, seen my pretty dress and fixed hair and that I was, after all, someone to dance with. The air seemed suddenly violet and light, and I put my arms around his neck and vibrated with happiness. He put his twelve-year-old arms around my waist, and we swayed silently to the heart-sending rhythm of "I Swear." But when I looked up, one of his friends was making a face at him, and he said in a voice loud enough for anyone to hear: *I had to. Mr. Wong told me to ask her.* And then he shrugged his shoulders and sort of laughed. And all my organs fell into my feet.

When the song was over, I wobbled outside, back into the dark, hot air, with the stars in their thick coats of water, and the ocean a black mouth out there somewhere.

•

For seventh grade, my parents moved me to Saint Anthony's, a private Catholic school. I was one of a few white kids in my class. The ideal look in the '90s in Hawaii was a mix of Pacific Islander (the requisite element) and maybe Japanese. Lean and almond skinned. Sleek black hair. So I spent recesses hiding in a bathroom stall.

After the first week, I learned to pull my feet onto the toilet seat to avoid detection, though sometimes girls would peer through the door cracks and laugh at me. When recess was over, I went with the rest of them back to class, praying that the teacher would already be in the room. If he wasn't, it was still open season.

Once, my science teacher caught me carving the word "fuck" into my desk and sent me to the principal's office. Soon after that, I was moved to Carol's school.

Redemption Academy was a fundamentalist school—the kind where they watch the *Left Behind* movie series and learn that the world is only six thousand years old and that carbon dating uses rocks to date rocks, which, they say, is a kind of demonic circular logic that proves nothing. At a girls-only assembly, once, we learned that we shouldn't wear bikinis or other immodest swimwear because our bodies belonged to our future husbands, and we weren't to give anyone else visual access to his private property.

Carol and I didn't talk about God. I didn't ask her what she thought about God letting her fester inside her skin cage. I didn't ask if she was mad about the raw, unrelenting pain of her life—the way she couldn't ever quite blink because the skin around her eyes was too tight, or the giant yellowed flakes on her scalp that prevented her hair from growing. I don't think that sort of thought was conceivable for either of us then.

I did not make friends at Redemption, either. Between my constant arguing with the teachers, which the other students found absurd, and the perennial problem with my pale freckled face, I was sent to the periphery again—less violently but just as absolutely. Even Carol, a grade ahead of me, avoided eye contact at assemblies.

•

I used to watch the other girls—how unselfconsciously they moved, they sat, they crossed or uncrossed their legs. I watched and moved a binder onto my lap to cover the wider spread of my thighs. It started in third grade. I remember sitting on the toilet and suddenly, looking down, realizing that my legs didn't look like other girls' legs. Of course, it took time for the worm of it all to settle in—but probably not as much as you'd expect. My mind began to wander over my body, crawling its surface to see where and how it went wrong. The weight of my mind on my skin grew heavy until I was no longer a child running down the street in freedom and simplicity. By the fourth grade I'd become something else. My mind circled back and back toward myself, venturing out to test the world, then scurrying inward again. *Incurvatus in se*, Augustine wrote some 1,600 years earlier—the human mind curved toward itself. Which is not what it was made for, apparently, and which may explain why, from those early days on, my body felt like an ornamental sack I had to carry around. But it was a disease of the mind, not the body.

And so, it wasn't in Monterey that my relationship with food was deformed—it's just that's when the deformity found a new expression, an expression that looked and felt like a way out, a way back to the garden of unencumbered limbs, freedom, a body so lithe I could afford to look out again.

•

But those two years in Hawaii weren't only miserable. After the earthquake of Mom's brief departure, everyone in our family was a little blissed out by the simple fact that we were all together—all four of us strange and sort of embattled in a world that didn't understand us.

Most days after school, my mom walked with me on the narrow beach near our house. I kicked seaweed as I told her about my many anguished desires and frothing fear and self-loathing. She listened and offered incoherent and obviously useless encouragement, explaining over and over again that even though seventh grade might feel like the most important year of my life, it wasn't. *Things will change, honey. You'll change.*

And we were great eaters. At least my dad, brother, and I were. When we ate out (which we did frequently), Mom stoically ordered salad after salad, while the rest of us ordered great heaping plates of pad Thai and bowls of udon, pizza, poi, burgers, sushi. We were the best versions of ourselves while eating. Noodles slapped against our chins as we made wonderful fun of each other and belly laughed and debated the bombing of Hiroshima until we realized the restaurant was empty. The waitstaff would be sweeping up and glancing at their watches as we licked our bowls and laughed, wiping tears from our cheeks. Then the four of us would pile into the car and nod our sleepy heads all the way home.

•

The other thing to know about Hawaii is that there are sharks. If you leave the sidewalks and their canopies of broad palm. If you leave the restaurants serving macadamia-nut pancakes and sushi. If you wander toward the sea and get into the salt and let the waves tumble you like a washing machine, and if then you swim out past the break, you'll be in tiger shark country. Out there, humans are mistaken for sea turtles. Or not mistaken. The tiger shark is second only to the great white for fatal attacks on humans. Aggressive, lean, cold, and dead-eyed. The Hawaiians call them *niuhi*, or "man-eating shark."

Sometimes a wave comes up on shore and grabs a person, like a great hand or a god—just scoops them up off the sand and lets them go in deep water. Sometimes a boy watches his father get pulled out to sea like that. Sometimes a girl is last seen collecting mussels from rocks. Or a man paddling his fishing rig out past a little peninsula. And then, days or months later, the lower body is found in a tiger shark's stomach, along with parts of a rubber tire, a tin can, and fish skeletons.

It used to be that when a victim was white, some Hawaiians would argue that the shark could not be caught and killed. Some sharks, they said, were *aumakua*, guardian angels sent by their ancestors.

•

That was the year my dad took me to scuba diving lessons. We were going to get certified together. I was twelve, the minimum age. In class, I learned not to hold my breath coming up from depth because the compressed air would make my lungs explode. I learned about not running out of air and the currents and a special, underwater sign language. We practiced in a pool, which was just exciting enough for me. I did not want to go into the sea. There was too much out there. Too much unknown and uncontrolled. Things that lived without light. I did not want to go down there.

But I did. I flipped backward off a boat into the too-living water (I'd heard that one cup of ocean water held some small particle of every creature that had ever lived—dinosaurs and cavemen and Jesus and Hitler—all in one gulp of fish-poop water). And we checked our equipment and made the signs and followed a little rope down.

I knew what I knew about sharks. But I followed Dad into the pit of my fear. He caught a baby octopus and put it in a little sack after showing me its astoundingly liquid body. And we swam around coral and schools of wild orange and iridescent fish and then touched our feet to the foreign sandy ocean floor and moonwalked before jumping up, as though we were birds or astronauts, and the light came filtered down in a wonderful tangle of radiance. And it seemed worth it to me. The possibility of dismemberment by someone else's guardian angel was a small price to pay for a kaleidoscope of wonder and flight.

# 8

# Darmstadt, Germany

*Does not man, perhaps, love something besides well-being? Perhaps he is just as fond of suffering? Perhaps suffering is just as great a benefit to him as well-being? Man is sometimes extraordinarily, passionately, in love with suffering, and that is a fact.*

Fyodor Dostoyevsky, *Notes from the Underground*

I hadn't especially wanted to go. I wasn't interested in promotion. But someone higher up put me on a list, and off I went to the PLDC.

Large green duffle bags at our feet, we stood awkwardly on a wide, empty road. Infantry. Military intelligence. Military police. Clerks. Cooks. And then there, at the far end, stood the Russians laughing. It was the first joint training of its kind, Russian and American enlisted soldiers.

Soon, the drill sergeants came out yelling. We dumped our gear on the asphalt and accounted for everything: Kevlar, the right number of socks, canteens, flack vests, underwear. It is strange that even now, some twenty years later, I have nightmares about being called back to serve. There's a war and the air is filled with smoke, and I can hear machine guns firing nearby—only I don't have the right gear. I'm out a flashlight or boot or something and am rendered useless. Worse. Somehow that failure always means we are going to lose the war. I forgot my socks; now everyone is going to die.

But no one died that day. Instead, those of us who were Russian linguists were each paired with a Russian soldier. We were meant to translate and would stick with our Russian throughout the month-long training. I was assigned a soldier named Grisha (Russian for Gregory), and unlike some of the other soldiers, he didn't smell bad. He had beautiful dark hair and was full of mischief.

The rest of the class was made up of soldiers from American units spread around Europe, many of whom had been deployed to the sandbox. In those days, we all had little flip phones that stored low-resolution images, and the infantry soldiers would sometimes pull out their phones when they got talking about Afghanistan and show us pictures of mortared houses and large-eyed, dirty kids and charred body parts. They never cried.

The Russian soldiers were also infantry. They, too, had seen war, but they were not like the American boys, who seemed young and breakable. There was something harder about the Russians, as though they had been born into brutality, and war was just a natural extension of their lives—not worse, not better. They laughed when our drill sergeants made us drink water during training exercises. They had trained to endure long periods of dehydration. They mocked our camouflage and the noise we made walking through the forest.

They had been to war in Dagestan and Chechnya. But it wasn't just that, because our boys had been to war, too. The Russians seemed like people for whom cruelty was the rule and not an occasional bureaucratic necessity. Even Grisha, who was smart and quick to laugh, had eyes that turned cold, and sometimes I wanted to kiss him back from whatever depth he'd traveled to.

It's one thing to be a part of a world that hates war but asks you to fight it, so that a part of you knows all along that it's all wrong. And another thing when that war is so deeply embedded in your people—the terror and gulags and bread lines, millions dead in prison camps for telling the wrong joke, women and children reported by neighbors, for what? For the Russian soldiers, it seemed that question, "For what?," had faded entirely out of relevance, out of meaning.

•

It must have been 2004, summer, when the Army sent Saul and me to Russia. (The details of the trip must remain unclear, but believe me when I say the mystery obscures absolutely nothing you'd find interesting.) I almost didn't go. If it hadn't been for Saul running me down one day on the parade field, demanding that I get my visa sorted out, I would have stayed inside the concertina wire. They wouldn't send Saul alone, but I was so caught up in the internal war, all my energy spent carefully managing exercise and food and recovering from weekend drunkenness. It seemed to me I could not possibly go to Russia until I had finally won out against myself. Once I drank the right amount and ate the right amount and ran the right amount, I would have the time and mental freedom to travel or look up or think of anything really beyond the myopic scene. *Incurvatus in se.* Poor Saul, I nearly robbed him of that trip.

But he did find me and was sufficiently angry with me, so that I went to the Russian embassy and got the stamps I needed and filled out all the forms. And then we were off. North. To the country of bears and monks chanting on wooded *ostrovs*, Saint Basil's and Lenin and little dachas where people lived in the summers and fished and gathered mushrooms with long sharp knives.

•

We took a cab from the airport in Moscow. Outside was gray, just how you'd imagine it. And there were holes in the roads, some as wide as cars. An Orthodox cross hung from the cab's rearview mirror, it bounced and swung, and I watched it make little arcs across the sky. Saul and I tried our Russian on the driver, but he, like most Russians we would encounter, found our misuse of his language offensive. He shook his head and grimaced and only sometimes laughed at our mistakes. We soon fell silent and watched the city recede into the distance, and then there were tall yellow weeds and abandoned cars by the side of the road. And for a long time it was like that.

Eventually we arrived in ———. I was dropped off first. Above me towered concrete, Soviet-era apartment buildings, each eight or so stories tall. They were organized around a series of little courtyards. Each of the buildings looked out at a small patch of grass, sometimes a playground. And all around the buildings stood with their hundreds of little windowed eyes looking down.

Outside of one apartment building, a small, blonde woman met me. Olga, she introduced herself. *Ochen' priyatno*. I followed her into the building and up many flights of dark, concrete stairs. It smelled of cat piss. Inside, her apartment was lit orange and yellow. There was a couch and a TV and a small balcony, one bathroom, a closet of a bedroom, and a white kitchen. The whole space couldn't have been more than six hundred square feet. She lived there with her daughter, Elena.

When I learned that I was to sleep in the only bed, I objected. But she wouldn't have it any other way. She and Elena would sleep on the fold-out couch. And besides, she told me, Elena spent most of her time with her boyfriend or at their dacha in the country. And so I put my things on the bed and felt very shy.

In the mornings, Olga served me blueberry blini or cheesecake. She'd heard that Americans had a rich diet. Sometimes she told me about her daughter, how she drank only olive oil and ate very little food and was therefore beautiful. And she was. It was one of the first things I noticed about Russia. Nearly all the women I saw were either stunning or toad-ish. There seemed to be no in between. I looked at my own round, Anglo face, my invisible eyelashes and muscled legs and felt with absolutely certainty that I did not belong.

After breakfast, I got out my map and followed it over to the center where I was to study for the next month. There were green walking paths and little shops and the horse-sized potholes I'd already grown used to. I noted a grocery store along the way and wondered if I was supposed to buy my own food or chip in for groceries. Anxiety.

What would they serve me? How could I run it off? I saw no one in running shorts. No one exercising.

Finally, I stopped in front of a stout, tan building. I walked up the steps and through a glass door. There was a short entryway lined with mirrors. I was bathed in peach, reflecting light. Ahead of me, a plump, older woman sat behind a desk. She examined me as I approached and made a slightly disapproving face. But I asked her the way to ———. Center, and she breathed a sigh of relief. She was the manager of a marriage arrangement service, she explained. A mail-order-bride company. And then she pointed up. Second floor. I found the stairs and soon saw Saul sitting at a desk talking to a State Department guy. Saul was already in love with the daughter of his house mom.

In the days that followed, I met a certain kind of Russia. The average citizen was by degrees tougher and colder than most Americans I knew. During breaks between classes, I went out front to smoke cheap Russian cigarettes. Many days, there was a woman there, also smoking. She was about my age with short blonde hair. She smoked beautifully, so that I found myself copying her gestures.

She was waiting for a husband, she explained. All the good men had been killed off in the Great War, as they called it. So now there was a surplus of women. It was a buyer's (husband's) market, and so it was pretty standard for Russian women to have many degrees and work as teachers or chemists or authors and raise children and clean and cook and remain exceedingly beautiful. But the men are useless, she said. They beat their wives for no reason. And then they spend days down by the river drinking *pivo*. Sometimes they might take a crack at fixing a car. *No*, she might have spat if she weren't so refined, *any American man would be better*.

•

In Russia, I learned to swallow *salo*, raw pork fat, with vodka. A little slab of it down the throat to slow drunkenness. We Americans visited underground dance clubs and outdoor bars, blue-lit and chrome. The theme was always discotheque, always ultramodern, a parody of '90s American techno. And when I drank, which I did often, there seemed to me something dangerous in the Russian atmosphere—a kind of ambient cruelty, as though there were no safety net, no reliable person to set things right. The police were corrupt. The whole country covered in scar tissue, callous, so that anything became possible. Only drunkenness brought me this thought. When I was sober, I thought I was the reliable person. But at night I danced with drunk Russian men and trod awfully close to something that felt like an abyss.

•

Speaking a foreign language in a foreign land is exhausting. And when I went home, there was no place to hide. Olga found me strange and was clearly uncomfortable with how much time I spent cooped up in the little bedroom. Sometimes she would invite me out to eat watermelon or watch TV. But I couldn't summon even a simple sentence in Russian by the end of the day. So, though it was rude, I hid.

And when I hid, I applied medicine to my tired mind. Out of my backpack, I pulled the stale and tasteless Russian sweet rolls I had purchased earlier in the day. Or small brittle cookies. And I ate them all in a numb trance.

Once, Olga went with Elena out to the dacha for a weekend. I had the apartment to myself, and so I tried throwing up in their bathroom. Only, the toilet clogged. In a panic I looked for a plunger. No plunger. I tried to scoop the waste out with a spoon into a bowl. Still, no flush.

Sunday night, I wrote a note to Olga about the toilet and stuck it to the bathroom door. She would be returning the next morning, while I was away. That evening, when I came home and dumped my backpack on the bed, Olga came shuffling into the bedroom, cackling with delight. She told me to follow her.

There was my note, stuck to the white fridge. Elena was in the kitchen, and they both erupted into laughter as she pointed to the letter. Apparently I had made an error, something about the toilet, only who knows what I'd actually said. Had I made a verb reflexive? I never did figure it out, but we laughed together, and it was the single happiest moment of that month in Russia.

•

I wanted to go to a Russian Orthodox Church. Naturally. My whole heart and mind longed to be in Christ's presence again. Is it hard to imagine? There was a girl riddled with disease and self-inflicted pain who also loved Christ. I loved him and did not know how to obey him. Later, I would know more, and my sin—to drink or starve or binge or lie or think only of myself—would weigh much more. But back then, I lived in a state of strange innocence. I sinned without knowing how not to sin.

Saul went with me. I did not have a skirt, and so I didn't wear one. But I had a head covering and went in with my head draped in a beautiful blue scarf. We lit candles in the narthex and kissed icons of Christ and the Theotokos and then stood in the back. No pews. The belly of the church, the nave, was dark—lit only by beeswax candles. Incense wafted slowly up, the air moved by our exhaled, singing breath. I did not know the Old Church Slavonic used in Russian liturgies, but some of it I understood or thought I did. *Gospodi pomiluj*, Lord have mercy. Or more literally, *Lord, cleanse me*. Again and again, I pleaded for his mercy along with the Russian faithful. But I still did not understand the mercy of God or what I was asking for. I thought, then, that asking for mercy was mostly an acknowledgment of sin. How awful I am, Lord. Can you bear it, Lord? Will you make me good enough, Lord?

Only a decade later would a priest finally explain to me that asking Christ for his mercy meant asking for *him*. Draw near, Lord, we might as well say. Come, be with me, despite everything. The mercy is his presence. I wept then, as a curtain of shame fell away from me. But that was much later.

After the service, several Russian women approached me to say hello, I thought at first. But they scolded me for what I wore, and looked disapprovingly at Saul, as though they knew about something between us. And the priest, when I kissed the cross he held, would not look at me.

•

When I arrived at PLDC, I was the fastest girl. It meant something. The drill sergeants seemed ready to forgive my errors and put me in leadership positions I hadn't asked for. And there was something else. One day, a drill sergeant walked into our barracks room, a room with ten bunks for ten women. When he saw me standing in a corner, he asked me to let my hair down, and I did. He looked at me awhile and then walked out.

Each morning I ate a half cup of cottage cheese and a piece of fruit. In the afternoon, a salad. In the evening, a salad. No dressing. *I like the taste of the vegetables*, I said. I got faster. Soon, I was faster than most of the boys. Two miles in 13:00. Two miles in 12:15. At night I lay in bed lusting for hamburgers. The salty meat, pink and juicy, thick slabs of cheese, forget the lettuce. But I ran my fingers over my ribs and sharp hip bones and the deep hollow of my stomach and felt something like purity, something like absolution. Triumph. Self over self.

Before too long, it became clear that several boys fancied me. They circled me and told me jokes and flattered me. I hadn't grown up with that kind of power, so I didn't show the right kind of indifference. Instead I drank it all down like they were just who I'd been waiting for. It was, after all, just what I'd been waiting for. I was beautiful, so small and irreproachable. And what I'd always imagined to be true for beautiful women was true for me, in fact.

•

During PLDC navigation courses, we used coordinates and compass and topographic map to find small objects hidden in the forest. During artillery exercises, we walked with the butt of our M16s in our armpits, scanning the foliage for the enemy and thinking about what kind of cover the landscape offered, and then a shrill sound would ring out. *Incoming!* someone screamed, and we all ditched the road for cover and formed a perimeter and when it was clear we pretended to take stock of the damage. Who was dead? Who injured?

We studied leadership and weapons systems and why a sergeant might use one kind of formation in an urban setting and another in the forest. How does a person command respect? Who can lead other people to die? It is an honor to be chosen, we were told. And so it was.

In the last week, we trained for the final exercise. We would invade a small desert village, occupying successive buildings until the mission, whatever it was—recovering a prisoner or taking one—was complete. Each of the four platoons was going to be graded against the others. We started early in the morning. Our squad was first in, right flank. One boy carried the M249 SAW. I carried the radio pack. We also carried M16s and wore flack vests and Kevlar, our water bottles bouncing awkwardly at our hips.

Hidden by foliage, we could see the adobe houses below us. We were supposed to skirt the tree line and then charge to the back of the first house. We would enter through a window. Of course, there would be real people positioned throughout the town as enemy combatants and civilians, so the first guys in had to clear the building, shooting only those who held weapons, sparing the others, before the rest of us followed.

I was terrified of messing something up. *What if I trip and someone gets shot helping me up? What if the radio pack catches on the window?* To my left, the grassy hill was covered in tiny white daisies. Then our squad leader got the signal, and we started running. As we approached the house I kept looking over at the wide-open, uncomplicated hill of grass. So green. I had an overwhelming urge to drop the pack. Someone shoot me, I prayed. Then I could lie down in the morning dew and look up at the clouds.

But no one shot us. We reached the back of the house, and in I went through the window. Everything went as planned, and everyone was proud that day. Except I knew what a coward I was and that when the time came, if it came, I would choose the daisies.

•

None of us expected it. The kid who was supposed to graduate at the top of our class was injured and couldn't complete PLDC. Then the drill sergeant who liked my hair called me into his office and told me that I was going to be made the Distinguished Honor Graduate. *How?* I asked. It didn't seem plausible. I hadn't been in a combat zone. I was not particularly skilled at navigation or leadership or marksmanship. *It's your PT score,* he said. *And you did fine in all the other courses.*

Baffled but pleased, I left his office. Soon word got around that I would be replacing the injured kid. Distinguished Honor Graduate was a high honor. He or she was supposed to stand for all that was excellent among NCOs, the enlisted class of leaders, "the backbone" of the Army. I hadn't known the other guy well, the rightful honoree, but I knew he was a large, muscled guy with brown skin and warm eyes. He'd been on several tours in Afghanistan, and he led with a calm, dignified voice.

Of course, there was dissent. The DHG was supposed to carry the unit guidon, or flag, when we marched. But when I lifted the heavy pole, a tall blond boy broke formation and ran toward me, ripping the guidon from my hands. I couldn't outpower him, so I receded to the rear of the formation. There, a few of the boys from my platoon said they would stand by me if I wanted to take it back, and so we ran forward, and I demanded the flag back. It turned out that only a few jeering boys supported the rebellion. The flag was returned, and I called bluesy cadence—not at all what they wanted, but what I wanted.

•

There was a time, then, a very brief time, when I was the poster child of the Army in Germany. Because of the special nature of our class, the joint, Russian-American training, generals traveled from all over Europe to our graduation. Even the Secretary of the Army, General Peter Schoomaker, came. And I stood in front of all of them and delivered a speech, and afterward there was a standing ovation. One of our toughest drill sergeants told me I'd be famous someday and asked if he could keep a copy of the handwritten speech I'd delivered. The next morning, I had breakfast with General Schoomaker and several other officials. No one really talked to me, except occasionally I would be asked a question, the way adults sometimes ask children questions in order to make themselves feel that they are good with children.

•

All the graduates had four days off after PLDC. A group of us decided to travel to Amsterdam. Two boys, another girl, and me. It was an eight-hour drive past Frankfurt and Bonn and Cologne. The wooded countryside whipped past. The windows down. Music loud. At one point, we stopped at a gas station, where I bought a chocolate bar. I meant to eat only a small square. But I'd been so hungry for so long. I ate the whole thing secretly in the backseat. And then, panicked, I asked the driver to pull over, and I ran into the woods and tried to make myself throw up. The others thought I was carsick, and I let them think that. But the sickly sweet of acid and chocolate coated the inside of my mouth, and I knew what was coming next.

Amsterdam was beautiful. Canals and light and tall, straight buildings along the walk. Fine, full-headed elms lined the waterways.

We found a hostel and nearby an American bar. The boys started drinking there and stayed for two days, only leaving to eat and sleep briefly at the hostel. The girl and I laughed at them and shook our heads, though I knew if she hadn't been there I might have stayed in the bar, too.

We walked and walked. There were the Anne Frank and Van Gogh museums and clothes shops, where Dutch women nodded approvingly over the way their clothes draped my bones. We looked at flowers and sat on benches to eat sandwiches. We wandered over to the red-light district, just to see what it was like, and I saw women in glass windows, standing or sitting. One of them had on a yellow wig, and she sat on the floor of her little stall and ate yogurt from a plastic cup, which somehow made the whole scene much sadder.

Then, at night, we found the boys and drank. On the last evening, I convinced them to go to a café with me. In the café I bought a joint and some mushrooms. We smoked the joint, and then we ran outside and opened our arms and flew down the street, as though we could take off into the black, weightless air.

•

After we got back to Darmstadt, the company commander called me into her office and told me I'd been invited back down to Grafenwöhr to attend a meeting of American and Russian generals. I was confused but pleased. *What for?* I'd asked. She shrugged and motioned me out with her hand.

I didn't bring an iron. That was my first mistake. So I was wearing a wrinkled uniform when I met the general. We were in his office, and he was excited about something. He'd just watched a video about Pike Place, the fish market in Seattle. He motioned for me to come around his desk, and he showed me the clip. There they were, men tossing shiny gray fish to one another. Everyone smiled. Sometimes they sang. Then the fish lay beautifully on ice—plump salmon with their dead fish eyes. And the general said that he felt that *that* is what is missing from the Army. *Look how organized and happy everyone is*, he said. And he played it for me again. *But we're not selling fish*, I thought. *And we're not being filmed.* He must have seen my confusion. His face dismissed me. I didn't get it. Then he told me that I was the best the Army had to offer. It was a condescending compliment. He didn't think it. Only, generals are sometimes supposed to say things like that to enlisted soldiers. Then he seemed to notice my wrinkled uniform and his brow furrowed.

After lunch, I went with the general and his entourage to a large hangar, where the Russian generals were to meet us. I stood in the back of a crowd as he spoke to them about tanks. A few times I was called forward to translate, but I fumbled a few prepositional clauses and kept asking the Russians to repeat themselves. They laughed and asked one another if this was the best Americans could do. I burned with shame. For dinner, I ate a salad made of lettuce and carrots and shrimp, no dressing, and then I went to the gym. And that was the end of the glory.

# 9

# San Antonio, Texas

*Who has twisted us around like this, so that*
*no matter what we do, we are in the posture*
*of someone going away?*

Rainer Maria Rilke, "The Eighth Elegy"

In 2005, my time in Germany was up and I was transferred to San Antonio, Texas.

San Antonio is a drought of a city arranged in concentric circles of increasingly barren strip malls and cracked pavement and heat. At the center of the city there's a river where green things grow. That's where tourists visit and the wealthy live. And standing in the middle of it all is the Alamo.

During in-processing, I walked from one beige building to another with a folder full of papers. The sun blasted me with a heat gun every time I left one blank air-conditioned outpost of bureaucracy and headed to another. I couldn't lose the papers or let them get disorganized. Some went to medical, others to payroll, others to clerks of different kinds. I needed to be assigned a weapon, new Kevlar, a barracks room, a job, a unit. The many legal documents detailing my military service, body fat composition, fitness, behavioral concerns, professional achievements and failures had to be added to a new filing system.

On one of my first days off, I drove out to look at the old, stone garrison. I was wearing white sneakers and sunglasses, looking up at the famous facade and watching people walk by in khakis, licking ice cream cones, making the peace sign and grinning at cameras. A block away from the Alamo stood a cartoonish, bawdy restaurant called Dick's Last Resort, a Starbucks, a mirror maze, and an aquarium called Sea Life, so that the Alamo seemed devastatingly out of place. A mere two hundred years ago, a dead body might have lain where I stood, and a great wild emptiness would have stretched out to the west and east and north and south. Just juniper and wild rabbits, rattlesnakes, dirt, the rolling hills and cottonwoods lining the Guadalupe River. And I thought about how that sort of thing happens all the time—that the Army and its wars were submerged in neon light and ice cream.

•

I met Raphael shortly after I arrived in San Antonio. It was early Christmas morning 2004, and a friend was driving us home from a party. We'd kissed at the party, but he'd slept with someone else. None of us knew each other then. That Christmas morning we stank with the same booze and were sick with it and carried the same, gross shame into that holy day—the despair of it all made sharper by contrast. I'd woken up under a pool table, tinsel wrapped around my neck. In the car, I learned that Raphi was Orthodox, too. Our laments synched up, and so when he suggested that we visit lonely folks in nursing homes that afternoon (as though we were not also lonely), I agreed. Something upright and decent. I called around and found a brown blot of a nursing home nestled in one of the city's outer orbits.

When we arrived we stood awkwardly under the fluorescent light of the common room. Red and green paper chains hung from the ceiling. A large crystal bowl filled with nonalcoholic sangria. Cookies. The residents seemed unfazed by our arrival. There was babbling and snorting. One man stared out the window. Finally, Raphi chose a woman sitting in a soft chair. Gertrude, she said, a former teacher. For the next hour we listened to her describe in excruciating detail how much she hated children. While she spoke, I watched the lipstick on her teeth and mouth, and sometimes my eyes would wander over to Raphi. He looked at her with such sober understanding, as though he loved her. Outside the nursing home, we laughed—but even then his laugh was charitable. And there were small coniferous trees and large white rocks and the winter sky far off and bright. I think that is when I fell in love.

•

Raphi was younger than me. Nineteen when we started dating. San Antonio was his first duty station. It was my second. I'd already spent a year in training and nearly two in Germany.

In the early days, he would come over to my apartment (we were stationed at an Air Force base, and the Army was compelled to follow their housing regulations, which were, without a doubt, sweeter) and we would drink and play chess and talk about books, and he would read me Charles Bukowski on my little balcony and I would read him poems I'd written. He loved me for the poems as much as anything else. I wrote one about him and he cried. I don't think it was any good, but we both wanted what poetry represented. Meaning. Beauty. Spiritual dignity. We were trying to work our way toward something human.

But that wasn't all. One night, he came home from the bar with the side of his mouth split open. He was very drunk, but I got him in the car and took him to the ER. When I asked how it happened, he wouldn't tell me. Ten stiches later, after sleep and aspirin, he touched his mouth gingerly and told me that he'd asked a guy to punch him. *Once?* I asked. He shook his head.

Meanwhile, I started a diet of protein bars, black beans, fruit, and alcohol. I threw up if I ate anything else. I ran long miles. I taped Mary Oliver's "Wild Geese" to the bedroom door and touched it in the morning. "You do not have to be good. / You do not have to have to walk on your knees / for a hundred miles through the desert repenting. / You only have to let the soft animal of your body / love what it loves."

It was, perhaps, the wrong poem for me then. I could never quite parse the meaning. It seemed on the one hand like terrible advice. The soft animal of my body loved alcohol and sex and too much sugar, or at least I thought that was my body. It didn't seem like a thing to trust. And yet, the poem softened the sharp edges of self-condemnation. It kept me from despair. It seemed to say that it was enough for me to show up, day after day. And so I did.

•

One morning, I called in sick. I wasn't sick. I coughed into the phone and heard skepticism on the other end of the line. After I hung up, I showered, ate fruit and a protein bar, dressed in civvies and headed out the door. I didn't know where I was going at first. My blue VW Golf zipped around San Antonio's great looping highways, a fantasy of freedom. Then, like a migrating bird, I was drawn without understanding to another climate. My blue whizzed over to the McNay Art Museum and parked. I walked under the hammer of sun into an old Spanish colonial building.

The museum seemed a kind of cathedral that day. As I wandered from nave to apse, I took in the brushstrokes and color and the artist's attentive eye. Human bodies, clothed and nude, laboring under charcoal, fluttering in canescent photography, submerged in plexiglass and velvet. My soul, or some other part of me, vibrated with the holiness of it.

I don't think art could ever matter more than it does to people whose sense of what a person *is* has been rubbled down. For such people, art has nothing to do with status or sophistication or wealth. It's about survival. That day I needed to know that there were people somewhere bent over tables and easels, people who cared about the mix of white and line and spatter. A kind of longing.

I drove home full of the illicit juice of it—the bright, directionless, unanswered prayer of the artist. There was no art on base, only function and functional symbol. An occasional eagle. The flag. Posed portraits of officers. Everything tan. Tan and black and Army green.

Once, when I was stationed in Germany, I'd planted some marigolds outside the barracks. It was just that nothing seemed to matter in that brown, drunk world, and then I saw them at an on-base strip mall with their orange pom-poms raised in jarring defiance of the Army's aesthetic corset. I'd wanted them to live. After I planted them, I left for the bar only to return that night to find that three soldiers had set up folding chairs around the tiny makeshift flower bed. They sat through the night with flashlights and whiskey guarding the flowers from the trampling feet of drunks.

But I didn't know anything about flowers, and a few weeks later the green stems browned and the proud orange heads dropped in on themselves and eventually to the ground.

•

The day after the museum, First SGT Finch called me into his office. *Kilcup!* he barked. *Were you sick yesterday?* I had hoped this minor infraction would go unnoticed. Of course, I hadn't gone to the doctor, and so I didn't have the form she would have signed indicating the truthfulness of my claim. I hadn't gone to the doctor because I was sick with something most doctors couldn't fix.

*No*, I said. *I wasn't sick*. First SGT Finch's face was red. It was always red. And fatless. And hairless. He had piercing blue eyes that gleamed because, apart from the red, they were the only color on his face. I knew he kept a bottle of vodka in the mini fridge behind his desk. I wondered if he'd had a chance to take his first nip yet.

*So you lied?*

*Yes.*

*And you're okay with that?*

*I don't know.*

*What do you mean, you don't know?*

*It's wrong to lie.*

*Yes, it is.*

*What did you do?*

I told him then what I'd done. He stared at me for a minute and then seemed to make up his mind.

*Let me tell you what you are, Kilcup. You're Hitler. Did you know he was a thwarted artist? That's you. You're a wannabe artist. A Hitler.* He spat as he said it.

I decided he'd already gotten to the bottle.

I spent the next two weeks cleaning bird poop off the barracks balconies with a toothbrush. My pay was docked, and I had another formal infraction, an Article 15, entered into my file. I didn't mind too much. Except when the wind blew dried bird-poop dust into my face.

•

Raphi had a good job. He had a mission, though he could never say what it was. It felt important, I remember him saying. Years later, I would walk with him on a beach near Santa Cruz, and he would show me a tattoo. Sixteen hash marks on his ribs. *For the sixteen who died*, he said. *Who died?* I asked stupidly. *They hit a house because of something I didn't read right. Sixteen innocent people.*

During that visit Raphi drank hard, like he wanted it to hurt. Like he needed his life to be deformed—how could he live otherwise? It wouldn't have done any good for me to tell him he was only twenty when it happened or that it was an honest mistake. Raphi wasn't that kind of guy, looking for a cop-out.

I was of no help to him. He told me about our friend—blond and tall, eyes slightly mean and laughing and full of life. Something happened, Raphi said. Last he saw him, they were at a bar in Austin, and then this kid took off all his clothes and ran down the street in his boots and dog tags. He was crying and then howling, and then he lay on the road waiting for someone to run him over. *What happened?* I asked. Raphi shrugged.

Every night, Raphi climbed the dark wooded hills behind his parents' house and sat at the base of a tree and drank his fifth or tallboys until a deeper black came over him. I knew it because it was how I drank, too.

But all that came later. Back in San Antonio, I rotated between day shifts, swings, and nights. Every three months, a new schedule. Sometimes the only light I saw was a suckling baby light, the sun just born and unaware as I drove home from work. And then there would be the darkness of sleep, and then the darkness of waking up.

On days off we hiked in the hill country and floated inner tubes down Comal River and went to house parties. Sometimes Texas lightning quick-snapped in the thick summer air. Then great, pounding storms would break the heat.

That year, I read *Drinking: A Love Story*, a memoir about alcoholism by Caroline Knapp. I don't know who put me on to it, maybe my mom. I remember reading about how she came home from work and drank two bottles of wine, and I thought then how sad it seemed—this single, middle-aged woman, so alone with her wine and her rituals of despair.

But then I woke up one morning and finished a half-empty bottle of wine and went outside. A dad was playing ball with his daughter in the apartment parking lot. They looked up at me as I squinted in the sunlight. And then I fell down the stairs. When I stood up I was bleeding from the forehead and elbow, and the girl and her dad were staring at me with their mouths a little open, or maybe that's just how I imagine it now.

•

I petitioned to leave the Army three months early before my official ETS date. Three months shy of five years. I'd gotten into the University of Washington and claimed I needed to start that January term, though I could have started any time. I just wanted out. Inexplicably, they said yes. So, in November I packed all my things into a U-Haul and hitched my VW Golf to the back. I had almost no money in my bank account, but I knew my last paycheck was about to be deposited, so I said goodbye to Raphi. I don't remember if we broke up or not or if we promised we'd call. But I drove away from San Antonio, its brown and empty trees, with a sense of conviction about the horizon.

I thought I'd head to Arizona, then take a northerly route up to Nevada and then jog west again. Eventually I'd pull up to my parents' tree-lined house in small-town Oregon. The sky was sheer and blue and full of wonder. I matched it. Heart blue and full of sky.

I was headed home. I pictured my parents' house on the corner of Ford Street. We hadn't spoken much over the past nearly five years. If we talked it was because I called. Sometimes one of them sent me a book. Sometimes I went home on leave (wherever home was then, Ogden or Juneau or McMinnville). Once I left, it seemed their lives closed over the space I'd vacated. But every once in a while, I would see someone wearing a Hawaiian shirt while riding a motorcycle, and my mind would twitch: *Dad*, it called. But it wasn't Dad.

I made it to Flagstaff that evening. High mountain desert. Blue and purple rock in the fading sun as I pulled into a gas station. I meant to fill up and find a place to sleep, but the pump declined my card. I thought about calling home, but my flip phone was dead. All of a sudden, I looked around and felt the expanse of space stretching out between Flagstaff and my parents' house.

Back in the U-Haul cab, I fished out my charger and my last four dollar bills. The gas station cashier was kind and let me plug my phone into the wall. Once the dull screen lit, I called my dad. It was like I was a kid again. Lost, scared. *Help*, I said.

I'm sure he shook his head, as I explained that I thought the Army had paid me. I thought I had more money. No, I didn't check. Yes, I drove off with a near-empty bank account. But somehow he got enough money to me that night for a little gas and a motel room. He must have heard the panic in my voice because he told me to meet him in Vegas the next day. He'd fly out and drive home with me.

The next morning I woke up with a fever. But I got into the truck and headed north. The barren landscape flickered out the window. Cattle here. A rising yellow hill. Jagged rock jutting at angles up and out. I was delirious, and the barbed-wire fences rolled by and the dust and wind.

Vegas is a strange country. So many ordinary folks living good, plain lives, their city rent right in two by the Strip, its cascades of light, fountains of it sparkling up. Neon flash and bang. Glitter. A river of fake hope.

I drove down the bright road and found the casino my dad had picked out. Neither of us gambled—it was just a cheap place to stay. I parked and clambered out, eyes swollen with fatigue, and walked inside to the dinging and trilling and red carpet. When I finally saw my dad, he was standing in front of a Chippendales poster. Four or five men scantily clad in black leather posed around his sober, bald head.

Glasses, yes. Flannel button-down, yes. Socks and sandals, yes. We rode the elevator up to our room and I cried and hugged him and snotted on his shoulder. I told him about the poster he'd been posing under and wondered if he was experimenting with a possible career change. His brow furrowed in disgust.

He patted me as we hugged and gave my cheek a little kiss—a truly stunning display of affection. After a brief chat, and despite the fever, I decided to skip dinner and order a bottle of wine. Relief, I thought. Dad murmured something disapproving or maybe just sad. And that night I drank my cheap Merlot and fell asleep and had no idea what my father might have thought, having flown all the way to Vegas to find his broke, sick daughter in a casino. It did not occur to me to wonder.

The next day, we woke early and got on the road. At a gas station just outside of town, we bought supplies: cinnamon gummy bears, sunflower seeds, Red Bull. I knew how to talk to Dad on a road trip.

It was the same kind of conversation we might have fishing or mountain climbing. Few words, mostly observations. An occasional question with long pauses in between thoughts. I made him laugh when I offered silly, intermittent metaphors—a truckload that looked like giant marshmallows quivering gelatinously up a steep hill. Or bad jokes about road signs or bumper stickers. Dad stuff.

The landscape undulated out our windows—all that dry, dusty heat and mountains far off, and then close. And the trees grew up coniferous and oak. We skirted the eastern edge of Lassen National Forest, then Shasta, cutting across the northeastern corner of California. Then into Oregon, my dad's gentle, amused eyes soaking up all that land. We rode the desert's back until the earth rose up into the air, into the Cascade Pass.

# 10

## Seattle, Washington

*The meaninglessness of suffering, not suffering itself, was the curse that lay over mankind so far—and the ascetic ideal offered man meaning! . . . This interpretation—there is no doubt of it—brought fresh suffering with it, deeper, more inward, more poisonous, more life-destructive suffering.*

Friedrich Nietzsche, *On the Genealogy of Morals*

The Army shucked like a dead skin, I felt sure I'd left my problems behind. My problem had been the Army—the prison of it, the incessant drumbeat of boredom and apathy, and then a shrill note running over everything: war, the waste of human life. If it had not been for that, I would not have needed to drink the way I had. If it had not been for the gross treatment of women in the military, the public weigh-ins and equally public ranking of sexual merit, I would have never thrown up. So when I was accepted to the University of Washington in Seattle, I imagined a completely new version of myself—myself in a place where things mattered, where ideas mattered and life would mean something again.

In December, three weeks after arriving in McMinnville, we packed up Dad's car with my few belongings and drove north again. This time along I-5 up past Tacoma, past Seattle's thicket of skyscrapers glittering to the west. It was a route we'd taken often in my childhood. Nearly every year the four of us—Mom, Dad, Henry, and I—would visit family in the Pacific Northwest. They were all there, grandparents, aunts, cousins, scattered among the dark fir and green orchards, godlike mountains and salt-wind coastlines.

We pulled up to a house on the north side of campus, the Russian House for international students. I'm not sure in retrospect how I ended up living there. I was not, of course, an international student. But we unpacked my things in the rain and cold, and I hugged my dad goodbye and this time he hugged me back and lingered a bit. It was the sort of ordinary scene that happens all the time—parents dropping their kids off at college.

Inside, I found my room, a cramped space with two beds and two desks. My roommate was not in, so I took a moment to study my new home. There were photos of her family on every wall, on mirrors and on the door, front and back. In every image, the face of one person had been cut out—the father, I thought—and sometimes a black knife had been Sharpied next to the missing head.

I decided to take a shower in the communal bathroom. My skin flowered in the heat. Pink and damp and wrapped in my old, pink bathrobe, I headed back to my room. But there were police officers standing in the doorway, and a small, dark-haired girl was crying and shaking her head. They asked me to wait in the living room.

Eventually, the police left, and I was allowed back in my room. That's when I met my roommate. She did not speak to me except to sort of nod, and so I thought I'd allow her what little privacy she could have. I dressed and said aloud that I was going for a walk and left.

The sun had set over an hour ago, and a fine mist of rain seeped from the black sky. I walked south toward campus and didn't mind how cold it was or that I'd forgotten a raincoat. The campus paths were lit by orange lamps, and there were tall feathery trees everywhere and then large buildings nestled in among the trees. It seems silly now, how much awe I felt. *These buildings are the houses of truth*, I thought with great seriousness. And then, less coherently, underneath that thought was the idea that scholars weren't the sort of people who would shoot someone just because they were told to. And the further idea that the roiling mess of experience in my belly, the strange and violent world out there and now *in here*, would be ordered, organized, given meaning somehow.

•

My parents had both attended UW as undergraduates, both the first people in their families to attend college. Maybe because he'd been raised Plymouth Brethren, my dad was first shocked and then enchanted by the world of ideas. His childhood world had been all-encompassingly pious. They weren't allowed to play cards or watch movies. No one went to college. His family was made up of hard-working, hard-loving people. They called their faith simple, and it was. They read their Bibles literally, prayed earnestly, and did not care for theological debate.

At first, his parents were proud that their firstborn son had gone to college, but soon he came home with new ideas. He started talking to them about church history, especially English history. He accosted his father with the superiority of his learning, and then, when his ideas were met with angry refusal, he fell silent. In the '60s he went to Harvard and launched a half-hearted rebellion against his upbringing. One half of him rejected and scorned the Plymouth Brethren. The other half never quite got over the beauty of that simple faith, its inelegant form, its plain and open-faced trust in a God no one seemed to care to understand.

But in the meantime there were conferences and scotch and books to read and classes to teach and tweed jackets to wear. Dad had broken out of the blue-collar world he'd been born into. Tremendous energy was needed to propel him into that loftier class, and so dad was busy with the business of "lift" most of his adult life—not material lift, but intellectual lift, conceptual lift—too busy to look down or back or under his shoe.

So when Dad talked about UW, it was with a kind of religious reverence. It was the doorway to real learning and depth, a place to discover the illuminated map of minds who had engaged with the problem of living, the problem of death. With this knowledge, a person might look out over the current landscape and see, I mean really *see*, the world in light of the force we call "God."

My mom's story was different in some ways. She'd grown up in a nominally Christian home. Her mom was an on-again, off-again single mother, who had a bad habit of marrying men as dysfunctional as her. But Mom's grandparents, who helped raise her, were Christians and voracious readers. Though they didn't get any further than public high school, they read Latin. Papa played the upright base. They were, in the best sense, educated, and they planted in my mom a love of learning. That, and by her account, she found reading the easiest and best way to escape the turmoil of her home.

When she got to UW, it seemed a bright city on a hill. She aspired to it, wanted to become everything that the university represented, to wield intellectual power like a fending knife. It was flight and self-defense and, I think, love.

And that's where they met one another, in one of my dad's History of Ideas classes. It was the '70s and so the students sometimes went over to my dad's apartment, and in low light they discussed Plato, Rousseau, Kant, and Nietzsche. And my dad poured nice glasses of whiskey and once someone brought a joint. My mom fell in love with my dad for being everything she hadn't had growing up. And my dad fell in love with my mom for being young and beautiful and smart—so full of everything that he was afraid of losing.

•

I started in winter term. I had a class on Russian military history and one on British lit and one on political theory. I read obsessively and spent hours in the Suzzallo Library's reading room. But the Russian professor walked back and forth in front of the class in a trance sort of mumbling to himself about the book he was working on. And the British lit professor was a young guy who was really into Cat Power and who didn't like it when anyone offered an earnest reading of anything. I remember turning in papers with Big Idea words capitalized, as in Truth and Knowledge and Duty. During office hours, my professor chuckled a little while pointing out the mistake. I burned with embarrassment, but what did I know? I'd barely graduated from high school, and the little I had paid attention to, Shakespeare and constitutional law, contained lots of capital letters. Why not, I'd asked? Why not capitalize them? He smiled patiently, but the grade on my paper didn't shift: C.

Back at the Russian House, I'd finally gotten a bit of the story from my roommate. Her dad was a bad guy, it turned out, though I never learned what earned him the title.

*Where does he live?* I'd asked.

*South Korea.*

*Huh. Did he visit? Was that why the police were here?*

*No*, she said, and then closed the conversation like a book. The pictures stayed on the walls, though from time to time they changed position. Sometimes they were all clustered over her bed. At night sometimes I woke in the dark to find her sitting upright in a chair, eating cereal three inches from my face. Other times she vacuumed at 2 or 3 a.m. I asked her once if she went to classes, because it seemed she slept though most of the day. She shrugged her shoulders and continued nibbling a Pocky stick.

It was a strange living situation, but I didn't mind so long as I could write and run. And drink. Drinking had been a problem in the Army, but that was *because* of the Army. Now that I was a student, I could have a few sophisticated glasses of wine, I was sure.

So I walked down to a little restaurant and sat at the bar with my books, *The Good Solider* or *The Protestant Work Ethic*, and drank deep glasses of Syrah. Between sips, I would write in the margins, underlining and shaking my head, until someone sat near me. At which point,

I often closed my book and turned to the stranger. I met Buddhist waiters and atheist grad students who pitied my faith, an elementary school teacher who gave me some stones she said would "ground me." I would nearly always get the conversation to turn somehow to God, and then we'd have a nice debate—the light swimming by that point, and then I'd stumble home in the dark and sometimes call Raphi and then collapse in a black sleep on my bunk.

•

Raphi had not been a casual love. During the first weeks we dated, I used to drink two beers before calling him. I'd have another in hand when the phone rang. It was nerves, my heart bounding around, distorting my personality. I needed sedative hops to restore me. We spent long hours on the phone talking about our childhoods and making dumb jokes and reading passages of books we loved to one another.

He chewed Trident gum and smoked. And so I started chewing Trident because it reminded me of kissing him and the time we listened to Van Morrison as we drove in this little beat-up car out to an old airstrip, and we sat there and laughed, and he unfolded a packet of gum and popped it in his mouth, and how happy I was by his side.

Mirthful Raphi. Coarse and funny and then underneath the jokes, a hard, self-loathing seriousness, an orientation toward suffering, an incoherent knowledge of the cross, and the heavy claim God places on our lives.

He was raised in a small Orthodox community in Northern California. Near his house, icons were nailed to trees, and he went to an Orthodox school and had been to Mount Athos. His brother was a monk there, and he used to tell me about how the monks smoked cigarettes and how one of them had a huge bag of Greek candies and would give some to Raphi every time he climbed up to the monk's cell.

There was a hard, no-bullshit love of God at the center of Raphi's world. And then, circling that adamantine core, an atmosphere of pain. I think it was the same for me. We'd gotten tangled up somewhere, each of us separately and then together. We'd forgotten about love and remembered only the painful beauty of Christ's face and the excruciating demand he placed on us. Having failed that—the demand—we threw ourselves into a kind of death, judging ourselves, thinking the judgment somehow made up for everything else.

I told him about the time I'd been at an Army training program out in West Texas, the desert and flat unyielding sky. How an Egyptian sailor had offered me Malibu and orange juice, cup after cup, and how he then locked me in his room. And how, the next morning, Sunday morning, after he had driven me back to my barracks, after he had hung my bra on a friend's door, I had run seven, dehydrated, hungover desert miles to the local Orthodox church and arrived in my running shorts, covered in dust and sweat, and how I'd stood in the back crying. And how the priest had refused to hear my confession and had instead confusedly prayed for me—clearly eager for me to leave. I told Raphi then how angry I'd been at the church. But now I see how strange I must have seemed. The priest and I inhabited different worlds, I think.

•

Soon after I landed in Seattle, I got a job at the university bookstore. It was a perfect job for me. I arrived after the bookstore closed and met up with a crew of other kids—a musician and a film student—and we each took a cleaning cart to our designated floors. I was a janitor, and I loved it. I popped in my earbuds and drove a vacuum through a maze of books, stopping now and then to read the back of a novel. Other nights, I took a rickety old elevator to the attic. There were offices up there and a giant grotesque mural of Charles Bukowski's face. At one desk, someone had carved faces into a series of small apples and then lined the apples up on a shelf. Every night, I saw the apples had withered more, so that over time, the carved faces bent in on themselves and the eyes sank and the facial expressions changed from joy to confusion or from surprise to despair.

I was often alone on a giant, dark floor, in a place that was obviously meant to be populated. No one was looking over my shoulder to see what I was or wasn't doing. It was like being in the zoo after hours or backstage after all the actors have left. I could move as slowly as I liked, letting myself invent stories for the people whose offices I cleaned or the people who might buy and never read Machiavelli's *The Prince*, and then also the people who did read it. I thought a lot about books in those days—the sheer volume of them, their occasional beauties, densities, failures.

I didn't mind the restrooms too much. Body stuff has never really grossed me out, though sometimes there was blood and sometimes poop and more often than I liked there were needles. Women's bathrooms attested to the sheer range of female experience—the kaleidoscopic nature of female fluids and their attendant odors. Men's messes, though more plentiful, were more straightforward.

Around midnight, after the trash cans had been emptied, carpets vacuumed, and toilets scrubbed, we exited the building into a dark alleyway. Sometimes a young girl was there. It wasn't a safe place, but she didn't seem to care. She crouched and looked at us and picked at her scab-covered arms and, like a frightened deer, ran away if we got too near.

•

Of course there were parties. College parties, frat parties, dumb parties with house music and kegs. But the kids in college didn't drink the way I drank in the Army. Or at least they didn't seem to. I couldn't relate to the students who had just left their parents' houses and were still titillated by a new sense of ownership over their lives.

There was something fresh and eager in them, a playfulness that I disdained. I wanted oblivion, darkness, a blank mind, not fun.

Sometimes I drank two glasses of wine with dinner while reading and then went to bed. Sometimes I drank two glasses of wine with dinner while reading and then found a group of strangers heading to a bar, and I would join them and then find myself, many hours later, stumbling drunk and alone in downtown Seattle asking strangers if they knew where I could find coke.

Once, I came back to my dorm room, where my roommate was miraculously in bed asleep, and I heaved myself up onto my bunk where I convulsed from alcohol poisoning until I fell onto the floor and fell into a dead sleep, face in a puddle of vomit. The next day I scrubbed and scrubbed but the acid smell of puke would not go.

•

As the weeks rolled by, I grew accustomed to the school's style of writing and began to earn good grades. We read primary, philosophical texts in political theory. It was the only class that really animated me, the only class that seemed to be asking the questions I so desperately wanted answered. What is a country? And what is a country for? And what are its citizens, and what are we for? What might war have to do with any of that? Or religion? Which are the bad ideas that sound good? And which sound bad but are, in fact, noble?

We read Marx and Hegel, Locke and Burke, Plato and Aristotle. But the thinker who stopped me short and who pushed my whole life in a new direction was Nietzsche. We were reading *On the Genealogy of Morals*. It was one of those books that puts a pin in a person's life and reemerges, year after year, as a point of reference.

Nietzsche's critique of Christianity, of bad conscience and slave morality, seemed to me a near-damningly accurate portrait. If I had not already encountered Christ, the reality of him and his burning, luminous love, I would have thought that Nietzsche's case was absolute.

Still, I didn't have the language to do battle with him in the margins of my book.

One day, I found my professor smoking a cigarette next to a bush outside the lecture hall. I walked up to her, uncertain how to put my question.

*Excuse me*, I said, *Professor So-and-so? I have a question about Nietzsche.*

She looked at me dubiously but allowed me to continue.

*Who says that he's wrong? I mean, who answers him? I'm a Christian and I don't know how to argue with him.*

She sort of laughed and said, *No one*. Then she picked up her bag, smiled patronizingly, and walked off.

I'm sure she believed it. Looking back, I can imagine how naive I must have seemed. A young girl who had grown up Christian and who was just now coming into contact with ideas that challenged her faith. But that wasn't my situation at all. I'd been in contact with realities that challenged my faith for years. I had, in fact, rejected the frail, morally inverted Christianity Nietzsche described—full of performative piety, false humility, self-righteous self-abasement.

There was something about beauty he was missing, something about the power and reality of Christ and the boldness required to follow him. But what did I know about it? My mouth opened and shut a few times as the professor walked away.

A week later, I switched my major to philosophy.

•

Once, I came back to my room and found a giant pair of sewing scissors placed precisely in the center of my pillow. A few days later, I came home to find my roommate's laptop on my desk displaying a series of images. In each one she was sitting on my bed or desk in her underwear.

After that, I called housing services and asked for a room change. I didn't really think she would stab me in my sleep, but I wasn't

100 percent sure. They moved me to Hansee Hall and gave me a discount on a single room, explaining awkwardly that my roommate wasn't actually enrolled in classes, and they weren't sure why she was still living at the Russian House.

A week after I moved, I ran into her in Hansee Hall. She was in the common area dressed in a ball gown playing the grand piano and singing off-key. I approached her cautiously and asked if she was taking lessons. She told me that she didn't need to. She was already very talented and was planning to go on *America's Got Talent*. She'd received word from God that she was going to be a superstar on Earth so that later she could marry Jesus and be a superstar in heaven.

I'm not sure how I responded. Not honestly, anyway. But I realized that perhaps the only difference between her scheme and mine was that my idea of heaven didn't involve *America's Got Talent*. I, too, if I had been honest, wanted to marry Jesus. And though I wouldn't have chosen the word "superstar," my real ambition, sainthood, connoted something of the ultrabright and celestial. If I had listened closely to myself, I might have heard how discordant my own note sounded. How off-key my life. It was the last time I saw her.

•

Living alone had its perks. No one woke me up in the middle of the night with their vacuuming or cereal slurping. No one took seminude pictures of herself on my furniture. It could have been a peaceful time. But there are many devils that thrive in privacy.

Alcoholism is one. Because there was no one to track the number of nights I came home drunk, I could fuzz the details, forget how often I'd been to the bar that week, forget even the pain drinking had caused me just the night before. So, during those months, I came home tilted and fell into bed with my clothes on. Or didn't come home, and no one saw it. The next morning, there was the grimy realization of what I'd done, but then came breakfast and then class, and by 4 p.m. the mess of it faded into a vague accumulation of bad feelings that led me to think a drink might be a good idea.

It's a strange thing, alcohol. So many people can have a couple beers with dinner and their lives don't fall apart. But at some point, I'll never be sure when, I crossed from being a person who liked to drink to a person who was spiritually dependent on it. I say spiritually because drinking was, for me, a spiritual problem. I didn't like who I was—my social anxiety and fear and basic incompatibility with reality—and so I altered reality. A shot of tequila was a doorway into another dimension in which I was beautiful and fun and at ease in the world. But the more I drank, the less I wanted to be sober. The more self-willed, the less a self. I moved away from God by inches, away from the person he had created me to be. After about three drinks, a crown appeared on my head. Two more, and I was the laughing empress of the realm. Only, it turned out to be a fickle, sad, and little kingdom.

Bulimia is another devil, an even more secretive one. The word "bulimia" comes from Greek and means literally "ox-hunger" (from *bous*, meaning "ox, cow, bull" and *limos*, meaning "hunger"). Cow-hunger. Ravenous. Morbid. Insatiable. What was I hungry for? What wasn't I hungry for?

I started bringing food from the dining hall back to my room so that I could eat while watching a show on my laptop and then quickly walk to the bathroom. Soon, it wasn't just meals but several meals at a time. The hunger in me at war with subsequent self-loathing. I remember the endless attempts to climb back on top of the horse. I established rules and more rules to reassert control. If I eat only fruit in the morning, then I can have half a chocolate bar in the afternoon. Or, no eating Tuesdays and Thursdays. Or, salad for lunch and dinner.

It was civil war. Self against self. Between violent drunkenness and violent rituals of indulgence and punishment, I plummeted. My mind and body seemed to shake all the time. I kept up with my classes but was inwardly dying. By then end of spring term, I withdrew from the university and moved back into my parents' house in the Willamette Valley.

## 11

# McMinnville, Oregon

*How can we not be dooms to one another?*

Iris Murdoch, *The Sacred and Profane Love Machine*

It was 2007, and I was twenty-three when I moved back to my parents' house. That summer, I helped my dad in the garden and went for for long walks with my mom. There were the familiar smells and the sound of my dad's quiet shuffling from room to room, his harrumphing occasionally as he read and my mom's bright energy and buoyant, fuzzy hair, her laughter and kind, unending interest in my life. We cooked and ate together. On Sundays we would drive an hour north to Saint Nicholas Orthodox Church in Portland and sing the liturgy together, so that something golden crept back into me.

During the summer, I worked at a local pizza shop. The manager was a Viking of a man, who I think hired me because he liked redheads. I started in the kitchen but frustrated my coworkers with my slow chopping. One olive at a time. Then I was made a delivery girl, but I had a terrible sense of direction. This was in the years before Google Maps, and it always took me twice as long as it should have to get pizzas to the right house. Despite my ineptitude, it all felt joyously simple and innocent, and I loved the rolling hills out my car window and the crisping of maple leaves and the golden slant of light toward dinnertime. "As kingfishers catch fire, dragonflies draw flame; / As tumbled over roundy wells / Stone ring," I shouted into the wind as I sped down Second Street. I thought I could be a creature like that, who "acts in God's eye what in God's eye he is."

In the fall of 2007, I started classes at the small liberal arts college where my mom worked in alumni relations. The campus was small and homey. Large oak trees lumbered over green lawns with walking paths between brick buildings. In one of those buildings, I sat in a plastic chair in a small classroom, my notebook and pen and books ready. The class was ancient philosophy. I didn't know it then, but I was sitting at the precipice of something. Not only of learning but also pain.

Our professor turned out to be a handsome young man in his late thirties. The students loved him, I among them. He was a charismatic lecturer, and when it came time for discussions, I think every single student felt that he somehow singled them out as being particularly insightful and interesting. He dignified our questions, while asking us to think more carefully, more precisely about our assumptions. No one was made to feel foolish, and so our conversation was always energetic, a current of excitement running through us as we grappled for the first time with ideas about being and time and the good life.

Of course, I had a crush on him. He was objectively handsome, and unlike my professors at UW, he thought I was bright, even reading my papers aloud to the class. My ego swelled under his admiring gaze, and I worked hard to retain his admiration.

Like most undergraduate philosophy students, I took myself too seriously, as though by reading Heraclitus and Empedocles I had entered a sacred and rarefied conversation, as though I were a real *participant* who had something to add. I remember walking around campus with other philosophy students, our heads bowed as we debated something *very serious*—at no point did we lift our heads and giggle at ourselves.

Then the professor invited me to join a group of former students and philosophers at a bar in Portland. I remember how my heart raced, how special I felt. The night of the gathering, I spent an hour in front of the mirror trying to adopt the look of a beautiful person so lost in abstract thought that she didn't care about beauty. Slightly tussled hair, only the most subtle makeup, mismatched socks.

The group met every few weeks and drank beer and discussed a philosophical theme—art or work or nostalgia. The professor's wife rarely came, but when she did I studied her closely.

She was Russian, a former student of his. She had delicate features and large dark eyes, and when she spoke everyone listened. It felt safe to envy her. It felt safe to fantasize about the professor loving me. They were married. He was my professor. Those facts stood like an iron gate around my lust, and so I let myself run wild within those walls.

•

The college was known for being a solid, middling school. Safe. Comfortable. The other students, who had recently left home, were into things like crocheting and playing board games. They were wholesome people, or at least it seemed that way to me. And I felt very far from wholesome.

I both envied and looked down on the apparent simplicity of their lives. What had they been forced to learn at gunpoint? Nothing, I thought. Not that I had either. Not literally. I'd waited in garrison nearly five years for someone to squeeze that trigger. But of course, no one did.

The truth is, I had no idea what any of the other students had endured. My projections were fueled by self-pity and a grandiose story I began telling myself about the depth that particular violence had given me.

But it was more than that. Though I'd been hurt in the Army, everything I'd endured had somehow *meant* something. It all fit into the great fabric of purpose the military had given me. I had burned with the intensity of the stakes: freedom, life, death, home.

But now the stakes were gone. Poof. And I wobbled. The implicit question of my adult life to that point had been, Are you ready to die—not theoretically, not spiritually, but by getting blown up? Then suddenly the question vanished into abstraction. In place of war there was Frisbee golf and grades and picnics on the lawn.

I couldn't sew the new life onto the old, and so there were divided, dissonant compartments. In one, Raphi and I laughed over bad coffee, but we laughed in the face of a chasm of fear and the sense of our lives burning briefly and ferociously out. In the other, I made a joke about the coffee on campus. And that was it. There was nothing behind it. Just a bad joke on a fall day, a day that could stretch out into many such comfortable days.

Only when drunk—blurry, rampaging drunk—did the old fire seem near. By fire, I mean death. And by death, I mean the glittering sense of life in its presence.

•

That first semester, I met a gregarious blonde woman, an older student, like me. Arwen wore bright red lipstick and heels every day. She was from Los Angeles, and stood out among the granola kids wearing Chacos and hand-knit sweaters.

Arwen loved people, and she embraced nearly everyone with the same warmth and pointed wit and readiness to laugh. So despite not looking the part of an Oregon college girl, she had many friends. And more than friends. She was married to a man who lived an hour north of campus, but they had a flexible arrangement. I listened with a kind of horrified fascination as she told me about the men she met at bars, the women she'd loved. From her stories I gathered that she didn't understand why everyone wasn't constantly sleeping with everyone else. It was all so casual and funny—just a little affectionate spice added to an otherwise milquetoast life. Arwen laughed at my discomfort with casual sex. A hang-up, she called it. But I admired her kind of love. It was simple and expansive and unafraid.

But love and spice were not the whole story. Arwen had grown up in a poor and wildly dysfunctional family. There'd been abuse of all kinds, she would tell me later. An uncle, in particular. But she made excuses for him and the others, even going so far as to say the uncle had done her a favor, though she had been a child.

The hardship of her life towered over mine, but we saw something in one another. Outliers, both of us. Ill at ease with cheerful wholesomeness. And though she mocked my artless clothes, and though I secretly thought she was sad, we became close friends, each pitying the other. Plus, we both liked to drink.

We danced in the speckled blue light of near-empty bars and laughed and did not talk about God. Her drinking was different from mine. It seemed organic and unforced—she'd been born into a life that demanded drunkenness. Drunkenness as a daydream. Drunkenness as laughing gas, as medicine, as the blanket you throw over the stained parts of your life. She wasn't out to burn herself down the way I was.

Part of the problem was that I still loved God. I wrestled with him in the bottle, or thought I did. Maybe an angel met me there. Maybe my hip broke. But the vacant place in my heart where God had once lived made waking life painful. And so I ran from that pain and did not know I was running.

•

Third Street was the center of town. It was lined with two-story buildings, the first floors of which were little shops and bookstores and groceries and restaurants. Above, there were apartments with large windows looking down, and there were trees along the sidewalks and iron lampposts, and bright white bulbs glittered above the street at night.

Right in the middle of it all there was an old brick building, a bus depot that had been converted into an eccentric hotel called McMenamins. It was full of eerie art and long carpeted staircases and secret nooks with little doors that opened into strangely large rooms. There was a restaurant and a cellar bar and a rooftop bar, where the light was orange and dim. From the rooftop, I could see the valley's soft, layered hills, the strata of watery colors that bled from sky to ground: lilac, bone, and fern. I read there and met with friends. Often, Arwen met me. She was in a lot of my philosophy classes, and we'd pretend to study until the gin got to us.

•

One day, the professor suggested we meet at McMenamins to talk about my upcoming honors thesis.

Sitting across from me in a booth, he told me how brilliant I was, how unlike his other students. He told me about his depression and how he hadn't completed his PhD in philosophy and how painful it had been for him—the feeling of failure that followed him around like a dark cape.

He used to be a near-Olympic-level swimmer, he said. I looked at him, broad-shouldered and long-limbed. There was something fluid about him, something that in certain lights seemed weak and in others powerful—like water, I supposed.

We began taking long walks together after class. He would drop his leather messenger bag in his car, and we would stroll around campus talking. Though now I can't remember what was said, in the beginning I'm sure we talked about the readings for class, then the personal implications of ideas, then our pasts.

I should have known what we were spiraling toward. But I didn't, or didn't want to. All I saw was that an impossible thing was happening. What had existed in my private world of fantasy was materializing. Still, I told myself nothing would come from it. I didn't know how subtly these sorts of things begin. I hadn't realized that it had stopped being innocent long ago. And so we walked side by side toward disaster, each of us reassuring the other in a thousand unspoken ways that the iron gate would stand.

And then one day in June, we sat on a green hill, and he told me my eyes were different sizes, as though it were a compliment, and then he put his hand over mine, and then I turned my palm up toward his. And that was it.

•

As soon as the vague idea of an affair moved into reality, a dark oil slicked over us. The corner of light in my heart blinked out. It was a little like the feeling of eating too much. It all looks so good on the plate, but once it gets into your mouth and then down to the belly, you're sick.

The professor grew erratic and obsessed with me. Every meeting brought new pain, but it seemed that we had to insist on our love—it had already cost too much.

A few months later, I told him that he had to tell his wife—not because I wanted him to leave her but because I was convinced she deserved to know. He did. And as soon as he did, I think, he saw plainly how his life had changed. And I began to see the far-reaching consequences of my selfishness.

I remember those months as a kind of dark frenzy. All the things that had attracted me to the professor vanished. His goodness, his humor, his bright energy. Instead there were stories, stories he told and that I agreed with, even though I knew what they were. He said we belonged to each other outside of time, that we were destined, on a cosmic level, to be with one another. The more he spoke, the more frantic and fantastical his stories became. There was something racing and wild behind his eyes.

Of course, now I know it was behind my eyes, too. It's the look of someone untethered from reality. My stories were not his stories, but they were still stories. I felt that *he* had started the whole thing, that *he* had made every advance. I minimized my role, feeling that I had been caught by a strong undertow and now found myself bewildered, out at sea.

If only he hadn't opened the door, I wouldn't have walked through. And now I was in a pit—a pit of pain inflicted on us and all those around us. If I believed the professor, we were destined for it and would remain in it forever.

•

In August, I decided that the thing to do was go on a long, bike-camping trip to clear my head. I got a credit card and bought paneers and padded bike shorts and a little stove, then I hopped on my Trek hybrid and peddled first west, out to the Oregon coast, and then south. I would bike all the way to Arcata, California, and then hop a train to see Raphi.

The first day I biked fifty mountainous miles to Lincoln City, stopping occasionally to pick blackberries on the side of the road, staining my fingers purple. When I arrived, my right knee hurt so much I could barely walk. So I hobbled over to a drugstore and bought a flimsy, Velcro knee support contraption. But when I told the pharmacist what it was for, he laughed and told me to raise my bike seat.

Then, I hobbled across the street to a restaurant where I ordered a few pints of beer and ate a fat burger, watching sunlight wobble in the old glass windows. The air had run over me for hours that day, scouring me. It seemed layer upon layer of grime had lifted off like great sheets and simply blown away.

But before peddling over to the campground, I called the professor and told him about the day, and as I did, the grime found me again. I felt heavy with food and beer and him.

It was still light when I set up my tent. Nearby, a wiry guy was reading. Turned out he was a grad student in engineering. I asked him about his trip. Where was he coming from? Where was he heading? He told me he was riding to the southernmost tip of Argentina. It would take him months, he said.

I told him that I was riding as far as Arcata, and he nodded. *We'll follow the same path for a while*, he said. Then he looked at my bike—not a road bike, let alone a touring bike—and then at the Chaco sandals I wore while riding. *Good luck*, he said and he sort of chuckled kindly. I remember being so grateful for that laughter.

As I turned to get in my tent, he said, *The worst thing about biking is when you're going downhill and the wind tries to push you back up. Don't you think?* I'm not sure what I said, but then I climbed into my sleeping bag and thought about that for a long time and then opened the book I was reading, which was, embarrassingly, *The Sorrows of Young Werther*.

•

The next four days, I rode along the lip of the Pacific Ocean, past sand dunes and marinas and stinking heaps of sea lions and fog-shrouded bridges. Salt on my skin, salt in my hair and eyes.

There was a flock of other riders that followed the same route, and we often recognized each other at campgrounds. But for the most part I was alone. And alone, far from the professor, I began to see with increasing clarity what had happened, what I'd done.

It was a mercy that God had given me the reckless thought of this trip. That he sustained me through it. Although I didn't quite think of it that way at the time, I had escaped the undertow.

•

Many years later I would read a book by Orthodox Hieromonk Gregorios. He spoke about necrosis, or decay, of the soul. It begins, he said, with minor sin. But sin is never content to remain minor. Its goal isn't for a person to get a little pleasure or relief, but for that person to finally become inhumane and deformed, an agent of chaos and disease in the world. The enemy's single-minded goal is the obliteration of joy and peace and, finally, life.

The first step leads to the second and then to the third. It's rarely a person's intention to become warped by sin, but that's how I found myself. Only an act of God could have spared me from what would naturally follow that despair.

•

I remember a sober friend once telling me about how she had left her four kids at a trap house so that she and her boyfriend could cook meth in a cabin high up in the hills of the Willamette Valley. Because she was high almost all the time, she spent her days patrolling the woods with an axe, looking for spies and cops. At night she imagined that her abandoned children were stuck under the cabin floorboards, moaning. They were dying down there, she thought, and were calling up to her. And so she spent whole nights clawing with her bare fingernails at wooden planks, her fingers mutilated and bloody by morning.

Then one day, the police did arrive. She and her boyfriend ran in opposite directions, she down, he up. She thought the police were behind her, and she stumbled frantically through the woods. All the time a cacophony of voices screamed at her (the voices were literal voices—she suffered from drug-induced schizophrenia) until she reached a bridge. When she was in the middle of the bridge, she heard another voice, clear and full of peace and authority, totally unlike the other voices that plagued her. *Stop*, it said. *Turn around.*

And so she did. She was arrested and spent time in prison, and when she was released she reunited with her children and dedicated her life to helping other women recover from addiction. *A window*, she called that moment on the bridge. And for reasons she couldn't understand, she'd leaped through it.

•

In Arcata I boxed up my bike and found a bus headed down to Santa Cruz, where Raphi was waiting for me, golden haired and wry and smoking a cigarette. On the bike ride down, I'd thought a lot about Raphi. When there were strong headwinds or brutally steep ascents, I'd imagined his face just at the crest of the hill or around the corner. He was a beacon of something good, something to rise toward.

But our greeting was strange. Raphi seemed far away when we hugged. As I put my paneers in the trunk, I saw a yellow sticker on his bumper that read "The Struggle is Real." That was Raphi, the struggle so deep in him he'd forgotten what he was struggling toward. On the way to his parents' house he told me about classes at the local community college, and how he'd gotten into UC Berkely. Environmental engineering, he said. He would be going to Nepal to help them develop a water filtration system.

He already knew about the professor and knew me well enough to know how much I hated it all. But he didn't judge me for it, or at least he didn't seem to. Raphi knew about sin, and so I think he felt sorry for me—the mess I'd gotten myself into. Besides, it turned out he was in love with a wild, curly-haired girl he'd met in Santa Cruz. She'd broken his heart. And so I realized that Raphi would not let me escape myself by running to him.

Instead, we drank and talked about the Army. He told me what he knew about our old friends, and we walked in the woods and down creek beds. I tried to kiss him once, but he kindly turned his head away. The effect of the whole visit was humbling. I didn't exert any power over Raphi anymore, but he loved me just the same. I think if he had responded to my kiss differently, I would not have believed his love, or I would have persisted in the mad fantasy that love was about sex, or that I needed to have power over someone in order to believe their love. That little time among the towering pines and redwoods and oaks, the manzanita and fragrant honeysuckle, Raphi traipsing along the dirt path beside me, the sunlight poking through the thick canopy, uncovered a buried sense of goodness much larger and sweeter than I had allowed myself to imagine those past months. Arwen was wrong about sex. And the professor and, most importantly, I had been wrong. My feet touched the earth again.

Humility is a word that takes its meaning from the Latin root *humus*, meaning earth or ground. The soil, its slow dutiful work, its frank solidity and willingness to bear both our feet and the light, the fruit it raises. I wanted what the earth offered and not the other—abstracted, lethal fantasy. And so without saying it aloud, even to myself, I resolved to go home and end things once and for all.

•

The story unfurled quickly. I told the professor that I wanted out. I'm not sure how I said it. Maybe I was too kind or too hard. But he did not or could not believe I would leave, and in the beginning I waffled.

But then he started stalking me, showing up at coffee shops and school functions he knew I'd attend. He'd lurk in the background, his high forehead furrowed and dark peeking around a corner. Soon,

Arwen confessed to me that she had been meeting with the professor for an independent study but that their sessions had turned into long discussions of how confused and heartless I was. He gave her one of his shirts to give to me along with a thinly veiled threat of suicide.

I told my parents what was going on. I don't think I'll ever forget my dad's face in that moment—a look of deep, penetrating grief. *Oh, Katie*, he'd said and then he was far away, inwardly digesting the new source of pain. Or first there was grief, then anger, then disgust—with both me and the professor. The college was my mom's workplace. She knew the professor well, and she cried over the tangle I'd made.

So, I found a room in a house down in Eugene. I'm not sure why I chose Eugene, except that it's where I was born. I moved down there and got a job at a coffee shop and traveled by train and bus to McMinnville once a week to attend classes.

The professor still seemed to know how to find me. He called me frequently, pleading for another conversation, thinking, it seemed, that if I would just hear him out, I would come back. But the thought of him, of what we'd done, made me nauseous. I was repelled, and honestly a little scared of him.

Sometimes I wondered if he might pop out of a bush and stab me. I had ruined his life and then left. *I* was starting on a new footing down in Eugene, but he was still living with a wife who despised him and teaching at a college he had once loved.

He hadn't been a violent man, and I had no real reason to think he would be violent toward me then. But he was teetering on the edge of madness, it seemed to me, unhinged, insisting whenever we met that I was still in love with him, narrating my side of conversations, grasping my hands.

My heart had turned into an absolute brick of ice. I could not be sympathetic, I felt, or I would get sucked back in. He felt that I owed him something, and perhaps I did, but I also felt that if I allowed even a sliver of affection, it would be translated into hope that I would someday return. But I hated with a cold hate what we had done together. He called it my "strange morality," which was fine with me. Maybe it was strange.

•

At one point, I started meeting with one of the therapists on campus. I told her about the affair and the coke and the booze and not much else. I registered her shock, but she must have checked herself because instead of acknowledging the severity of the situation, she accepted it all as a matter of course, affirming my feelings, offering no resistance to the self-serving garbage I unloaded.

But the stalking intensified, as did my fear. So that eventually, I knocked on the philosophy chair's office door and sat across from this wonderful, white-haired man, who seemed so noble to me in that moment, and I confessed that the professor and I had been in a relationship. I had expected him to maybe feel sorry for me, but instead he shook his head and let out a long and weary sigh. *Oh no*, he said. The school would have to conduct an investigation. There would be grief and anger among the faculty and students. It was a wide-rippling sin.

•

Down in Eugene, I became obsessed with the boy who held my face to the snake terrarium and who liked to watch movies about cannibals and who once laughingly threatened to kill me. Sallow-skinned and drugged out. I used him to punish myself, thinking it a kind of justice.

I never heard back from the school about the investigation, but one day, long after I'd graduated, my mom told me that they had closed the case. The professor stayed on the payroll. Mom said that the HR woman leading the investigation had conducted several interviews with the professor and found him sympathetic.

A few months later, I called Arwen. She hadn't answered the last few times I'd tried, but there was her voice, *Hello?* We chatted haltingly, awkwardly for a few minutes. I told her how the investigation had wrapped up. There was a long silence.

*Kate.*

*Yeah?*

*I need to tell you something. The professor and I are together.*

A faint buzzing started from the far end of the room. Was the neighbor mowing?

*How did that . . . I mean, when . . .*

*We just really bonded during the time you abandoned him. I was there for him, and we were always at the bar. Anyway, I left Bob. We're divorced, and I'm trying to be monogamous.*

*Oh.*

*And I want you to know that I defended the professor against your attack.*

The buzzing was closer now, near my eye.

*You what?*

Arwen had been my main witness. I'd told her everything. She'd heard him talk about following me.

*I told the investigators you were just resentful and trying to hurt him, which you were. You were so cruel, Kate. He didn't deserve that.*

*You lied?*

She was quiet for a bit and then said, *You don't have to like it, but it was the right thing to do. Have a nice life, Kate.*

The line went dead. The buzzing now filled my whole body. I looked out the window for a long time. Then I picked up my purse and walked down to the little grocery market and bought a bottle of Yellowtail and wandered over to the nearby park. I was still vibrating when I sat on a swing and unscrewed the cap. I couldn't feel anything except for the buzzing until I'd sucked the whole dark thing down.

## 12

# Eugene, Oregon

*All human nature vigorously resists grace because grace changes us and the change is painful.*

Flannery O'Connor, *The Habit of Being*

That's how I found myself in Eugene, sitting on a little bench outside an Orthodox church, feeling that I could not go in. A soft patter of rain fell, and the old priest came out. And there was the tea flower blooming like an underwater flame in a clear teapot. And the awkward gentleness of the priest's wife. And my dumb refusal to see any of it as an answer to the incoherently offered prayer I'd cried over just minutes earlier: *Let me come home, Lord.*

Those were the days when I walked around Eugene in a gross, blue sweater and did not exactly want to kill myself so much as sort of accidentally fall into traffic or trip and get impaled by a fence post. The days blanketed in hungover pain. Days of shoplifting food and showering infrequently and crows making their great swooping signs in the white fog outside my window.

•

Some people are purists. They are alcoholics or sex addicts or gamblers. That's the affliction and once it's gone, life gets good again. But I was not that kind. Instead, I had a rotating cast of addictions.

When one popped its head up, I'd wrestle with it until it receded, only to find another had appeared in its place.

In McMinnville, coke had removed the need for starving myself and so the whole war around food evaporated. That, and the affair was its own kind of drug, and a kind of god. In Eugene, I drank and stole food and threw it up and used men to both punish and console myself, though none of it worked.

Sometimes a wine bottle. Sometimes a new job. Sometimes a cleansing "fast." Sometimes, a boy, believing as I did that my life could disappear inside his. Sometimes coke. Sometimes weed. Sometimes I bent over a toilet in a self-correcting panic. Sometimes the deathward course of my life romantically lit up, so that it seemed the blinking stars applauded my self-circling descent.

I smoked American Spirits when I could afford them and anything else when I couldn't. On weekends I went to bars hoping someone would buy me shots. One week I spent my last four dollars on beer. How long did it go on like that?

The real affliction, the one I couldn't see, was Jonah's—I was on the wrong ship, heading in the wrong direction, away from reality, which is another way of saying away from God.

•

I started going to meetings in the fall of 2009. I remember showing up over and over again only to announce that I drank the night before. I was tempted to lie. I was going to get sober at some point. What would it matter if I just skipped this liturgy of humiliation and banked on what I knew would eventually be true? But at nearly every meeting I heard the same radical idea: I had to be honest. My life depended on it. Let everything else go to hell, just tell the truth, they said. And so I did. Week after week, I raised my hand and said that I'd relapsed.

Once a college friend came to visit, and we decided to go out to dinner. Of course, she'd wanted to talk about the professor. I dreaded it but felt that I owed not just her but everyone a chance to ask their questions. She'd loved him, too.

On the way to the restaurant, I told her I'd stopped drinking. *I can drive*, I'd said, and offered that she should feel free to drink around me. I think I had almost a month sober then. At the restaurant, she ordered a glass of house red. But as the waiter passed her glass in front of me, I got a whiff of acid and dark fruit, and she seemed so happy and kind of innocent holding the glass stem. So, I hurried to explain that I'd be drinking after all and called the waiter back.

That night my friend drove my car home by herself. Some other kids I knew had shown up and wanted to go barhopping, and I, already three glasses deep, decided to go with them and didn't notice my friend as she picked up her coat and went out into the dark alone.

•

Another time, I was maybe two weeks sober when I took the train home to visit my parents in McMinnville. My mom mentioned that a veteran was speaking at the library on campus. So I walked up to campus and stood in the back of a small crowd of people and listened to a young man, not much older than me, put up a portrait of military life—of mortars and the dead and young men sent to do it. He spoke about the bureaucratic structure covering the whole scene with its stupid and inhuman effort to make sense of it. He spoke about the astounding number of veterans who commit suicide every year. Of course, I hadn't been to Iraq or Afghanistan, but I had lived in the same world—the one that could make sense of killing children and turn a blind eye to rape and in almost the same breath unironically assert the high moral character of soldiers.

When I walked into that warm library annex, the Army had not existed except as a kind of faraway dream. But as the man spoke, it came ripping out of the shadows and into focus again. Something bound up my guts. Something else crawled under my skin, as though saying, *It was real. It was real.*

I approached him after the talk to thank him. Soon a group of us were walking to a bar, and because the Army was back, I had to drink. The next morning I was supposed to give a poetry reading on campus, but that Marine and I watched the sunrise from under a train trestle. There had been not just drinks but mushrooms and weed. I had a vague memory of crossing the train trestle in the dark the night before, leaping dangerously from one wooden plank to another right along the edge, and then there was the drop, a little sea of rocks below.

After he left, I walked back to campus for the reading. I was late and stumbled toward the microphone at the front. I hadn't slept and I was dirty and stank of sweat and alcohol and smoke and there were leaves in my hair. I think I imagined myself a kind of Jack Kerouac. To either side of me were clean, generous people who had taken time out of their mornings to listen to someone else read their poetry out loud. But I didn't care about that. I thought in that moment that I was the only one in the world who was really alive. And so I read my poems as though I were spitting at them, those kind, sane people. And then I stumbled out the door and was soon asleep on my parents' couch.

•

I think one of the difficult things to understand about the addicted is that they can love a person—a spouse, a child, a parent—while being utterly incapable of acting upon that love. That's how it was for me for a long time. I loved God but could not be faithful. I loved him, but the further I burrowed away from him into the dark recesses of delusion, the more I began to believe he could not love me, that I had been shut out. If he loved me, surely he would have sent an angel to pull me up out of myself by now.

•

In the beginning, I wasn't sure alcohol was my problem. It seemed like a subsidiary problem under the larger problem manufacturer, Kate Inc. So, I wasn't sure sobriety would work for me. I wasn't usually a daily drinker. I didn't have cirrhosis of the liver. I wasn't homeless. I was just messed up, and so I drank—or that's how it seemed.

But I kept going to meetings. At first, I went because even though I wasn't sure I was an alcoholic, I *was* sure that I liked what I heard there. The people were weird, rooms full of doctors and people from drug court and bikers and housewives all hanging out together, talking about honesty and God and how they had lost their dignity and then reclaimed it, people who laughed at themselves.

In one of my first meetings, I was called on to talk. It would surprise anyone who knows me now to learn that I was shy then. Everyone at meetings seemed to speak with such clarity and wisdom. They had access to something I didn't, and so I didn't know how to talk to them. What a mercy it was, looking back, to come into contact with something so simple and good that it baffled me. So, I said, *My name's Kate. I don't know if I'm an alcoholic, but I, um, have this hope that, uh, someday I might hope to, well, I don't know.* And then I stopped talking. And the people around me smiled as though I'd said something wonderful, and later some of them approached me and told me how welcome I was and that they were glad I was there.

•

There was a man who described looking at himself in the mirror before getting sober. The face looking back at him was not his own. He saw bloodshot eyes and an angry, lined face. He hated the man he saw. It was something I understood, hating yourself.

Myself was a coat I wore, something that wasn't me but was on me. I could take one coat off and put on another—now soldier, now student, now girl trying to be sexy, now girl who hated being a girl, now someone who loved God, now someone who ran from Him, now playing the part, now howling.

There was something underneath the coat, I knew. I just didn't know what it was.

In another meeting, a blonde girl sitting next to me passed me a folded scrap of paper. When I opened it, it read, *Listen for the similarities*. I was annoyed. Who did she think she was, offering me advice, as though I didn't already know how to listen? But she had heard me say that I wasn't sure I was an alcoholic, that I didn't seem to have it as bad as a lot of people there.

After the meeting she turned to me and started talking. She was six months sober—a whole eternity of sobriety as far as I was concerned. She was funny and smart, and soon I forgot how annoyed I'd been. It seemed she wanted to be my friend, and she invited me to go running with her. *Do you know the Amazon Trail?* she'd asked. There was a morning meeting nearby. We would go for a jog and then hit the meeting.

I loved her and loved that I was faster than her and didn't mind that she was prettier than me. And then one day, for the first time in a long time, I stopped thinking about who was prettier and who was faster. All that mattered was that we were both hungry for sanity and had endured many of the same humiliations. We panted in the morning mist as we galloped over wood chips and roots, and the wet trees hung down their dripping leaves, and a cold stream curled around rocks, and with heavy breath we talked about men and God and madness and the joy of being alive. And then, smelling of fog and sweat, we went into a little building, and there were people laughing down the hall and the smell of burned coffee. And though at first I knew almost no one there, I was home.

•

One day, I picked up a yellow, tattered book that had been sitting on my shelf so long I couldn't remember who had given it to me. *People of the Lie*, the cover read. On the back I recognized the author as the same man who had written another book I'd loved, *The Road Less Traveled*. M. Scott Peck was a psychiatrist who became a Christian in midlife. I flipped open the book. It detailed his clinical observations of evil, a whole category of thought that was scientifically unverifiable but, he said, existed just the same.

I did not put the book down again for many hours. At first I read out of morbid curiosity. But soon I realized I was reading about myself. Though the stories didn't match the particulars of my experience, I saw a thread of deception so deep and tangled that it had become a part of me. I read about the tendency of evil to produce confusion and chaos. My mind raced backward in time, searching for a time I had been an agent of peace or clarity. No, for a long time I had been a whirlwind of disease, my confusion spreading like a contagion. I didn't understand when people seemed hurt by me. I didn't understand why I couldn't keep a job or a relationship.

Then, I came across a story about a young woman and saw that I was just like her. There I was, sitting across from Peck, my own throat producing the words she said. Like me, she was smart and reasonably attractive. And like me, she failed at most everything she tried. And like me, she flew from state to state and job to job and when things didn't work out, she moved again—new man, new apartment, new clothes, new hair.

The problem, it turned out, was that underneath everything else, she didn't believe that rules applied to her—not even the basic rules governing things like time and traffic. She'd made herself into a kind of demigod, to whom reality was required to bow. If she were to submit to the conventions of the world, she would lose her special, rare, and lofty position. Wherever she went, she left a path of perplexity and pain, or, at the very least, disgust.

I suddenly recalled lies long forgotten, the pain I inflicted on people who loved me, sorrows, confusion. I drank and manipulated and bent the rules because all I could see was my small desire overgrown to fill the whole frame.

The organizing lie was this: I believed I did not belong to the world. I was to its side and was therefore not subject to its laws. I was not one person among many people, but an alien observer who could choose to see and unsee what she liked. I could lift the yellow lines off the road and swerve, and if I crashed into you—that was at least partly your own fault, I thought.

Blood rushed out of my extremities as I read. It was as though a veil had lifted and I saw my own face for the first time. I felt dizzy and nauseated and lay down in bed and fell into a fevered sleep.

When I woke again, I felt refreshed and maybe a little lighter. There was no bright light or voice of God or anything like that. But I think something happened that night. Something loosed or forced from hiding. I could not unsee my own spiritual nakedness. There was something in me that was quite ill, and it wasn't what I'd thought all along. Peck's portrait of that woman rang out like a clear bell over my head. I would have to abandon my small and stupid throne.

•

Around that time, I started going back to church on Sundays. A few of Will's old students had become Orthodox after reading the church fathers in class. I'd met them when Will and I were dating. After we broke up, the friendships had stuck. So when I walked through the doors of the Serbian Orthodox Church, I saw some familiar faces. There was the old priest with tiny spectacles and caterpillar eyebrows mumbling emphatically before the iconostasis. And there were my friends in long skirts and headscarves. They bowed and crossed themselves, and I joined them, and together we followed the movement of the liturgy as though it were a great ship carrying us over waves—up and down and up and down, we rose and fell. Dry, fragrant incense filled my nose and mouth. I didn't understand it but felt my sodden soul airing out. And the flicker of candles and the solemn sweetness of our song, *Again and again, in peace let us pray to the Lord.*

In January, I asked the priest to bless my house. I should have told him the kind of house it was but forgot to mention it. When the priest and his wife arrived, I showed them to the living room, where I slept. There was my mattress on the floor and a dresser where I kept my clothes. And next to my bed were the paper icons I had taped to the wall. The priest was startled. His wife seemed uncomfortable and kept correcting the way I spoke to her husband. But he blessed my room, at one point standing next to my mattress and flicking holy water at my icons and sort of shaking his head. It was all probably a little undignified for them. But I didn't mind. The memory of that writhing night was still fresh, and I craved God's presence enough to let them see my poverty. Chicken hatchery, tofu factory, nearly destroyed by anarchy. Holy, I prayed, let it be holy next.

The priest's wife asked me what we were going to eat. *Eat?* I asked. *Yes,* she said. *If you invite a priest for a house blessing, it's customary to feed him.* I must have looked bewildered. She looked at me sympathetically and suggested I might pop some popcorn. So I did, and we sat at a card table, and they pretended to enjoy the food I'd prepared for them. Because I'd been corrected so many times, I wasn't sure how to speak to them. I tried to think of a pious topic but nothing came to mind. I think I asked if they had children, and did he like being a priest? *Yes,* came his muffled answer between handfuls of popcorn.

As they were leaving, the priest's wife—*matushka* in Slavic tradition—turned to me and said that I would become more comfortable the more time I spent at church. My face burned a little and I nodded.

But the next Sunday I was there again. And the next after that, not because of the priest but despite him. It was as if, after a season of overcast, a few bright rays of light pierced the clouds, and so I drank what light I could from church and meetings and prayed at night. And God did not withhold himself then, maybe he never had. And the beauty of his presence shot through me again. How can I say it? Like a clean rain, an ascending scale, rhododendron in full bloom, or a cauterized wound—like love.

13

# McMinnville, Oregon

*And the Lord spake unto the fish, and it vomited out Jonah upon the dry land.*

Jonah 2:10 (KJV)

I am sitting at my kitchen table. It is 2024. Warm winter light spreads over the table, heating our Advent candles so that they begin to soften and droop. And the fiddle-leaf fig and the succulents in their pots reach for the sun and are pleased to find it. In one of the bedrooms, my nineteen-month-old is napping, his fatty cheek squished against the mattress, his fine golden hair in tangled curls. In another room, a fiercely imaginative four-year-old makes a truck city, an elaborate society of rule-breakers and rule-followers. His shock of red hair bobs over the miniature world.

Every morning, I love them. I make eggs and toast and fruit and put it on their plates. The boys are messy and wild, the little one tossing eggs onto the floor. The older one sometimes makes a show of his manners and sometimes spends the whole meal hopping up from his chair to run around the table and flick orange peel at his brother. And I love them.

My husband, Graham, is at the church where he works. He is a priest, but not the fussy kind. He chases me around the kitchen in the evening with a plastic spoon, thwacking me on the butt. And he makes fun of me mercilessly and kisses me, and we are great friends.

Our house is filled with plants because Graham keeps them alive. And it is filled with secondhand furniture I found online. And there are dirty dishes in the sink and unfolded laundry and bills I need to pay and little failures and little victories. But at some point nearly every day, I am shocked again by the miracle of it all. How did someone like me end up in a life like this?

Sometimes it seems like God plucked me out of my former life and deposited me in this one. But that's not how it happened. Nothing was forced on me, not even joy. I imagine God offering me little pieces of reality slowly over time, little crumbs of bread leading me through a dark wood. If I had seen it all at once, I would have despaired. But he was gentle and offered only enough to keep my feet moving.

•

In 2010, the rental agreement for the house in Eugene was up. My roommates were moving out, so I found an apartment a couple miles from my parents' house in McMinnville. The apartment building was a small, two-story, yellow building. A one-minute walk got me to Starbucks, where I had a job as a barista. And there was a grocery store just across the parking lot.

The first day I was supposed to show up for work, I overslept. My alarm didn't go off. I woke in a panic and called my new boss apologizing, explaining that I was sick. He said it was no big deal, but later that day I did start to feel sick. The lie soured my stomach—it was a new feeling. In the evening, some women I'd met in recovery came by to take me to a meeting in a nearby town. They laughed and chatted as we drove in the dark, and then all at once I blurted out that I'd lied. There was a brief silence in the car, and then one woman asked me to tell them about it. I did. She sternly told me that I'd have to tell my boss the truth. *But he might fire me!* I said, thinking of the embarrassment and then how I wouldn't be able to pay rent or eat and would have to move back in with my parents and how I'd probably end up living with them forever. *It doesn't matter, Kate. If you don't tell the truth, you won't feel at ease in reality, and then you'll end up drinking. Is a job at Starbucks really worth it?*

I spent the whole rest of the night thinking about it. It was a terrifying idea, and the lie seemed so small and excusable and like the sort of thing people did every day. But another part of me knew she was right, and so the next day I got to work on time and during a break I pulled my boss aside and told him that I'd lied. My face burned as I spoke. But when I was done he seemed to have only half heard me and said with a wave of his hand that it didn't matter because he couldn't have trained me yesterday, anyway. And then he showed me how to make a strawberry frappuccino.

On the near side of the confession, I felt telling him what I'd done might kill me, however silly that might seem now. But on the far side, after it was done, I felt an explosion of light. God was with me. He had given me the courage to admit my failure, and I was sure that he was at least partly responsible for the safety I felt afterward—I had not lost a thing.

That afternoon, I was working the cash register when, outside the glass door, I saw a host of house sparrows flittering around in the parking lot. Their small brown wings fluttering now and then as they pecked at crumbs. Then a truck nearly ran them over. *Only nearly*, I thought.

•

I'm not under the illusion that I'm more or less sinful than most other people. But I will say that I have a tendency to sin in very loud and socially unacceptable ways. No one gives you a pat on the back for stealing food or drinking until you puke or getting fired from jobs or having an affair. But I think that kind of sin is preferable (and by preferable, I mean easier to address) to the other kind, the sin society rewards: excesses of ambition, codependency that looks like a desire to help, preoccupation with being the good boy or girl, people-pleasing, some forms of vanity. It's a wonderful thing when society reinforces the wrongness of sin and a very dangerous thing when it does the opposite.

Once, I was at lunch with an Anglican priest, a good priest, I think, who scoffed a little at the general confession. I'd been praying the words every Sunday for a year. "Almighty God, Father of our Lord Jesus Christ, Maker of all things, Judge of all men; We acknowledge and bewail our manifold sins and wickedness, Which we, from time to time, most grievously have committed, By thought, word, and deed . . ."

*Who really bewails their sins?* he'd asked. *Who finds the burden of them intolerable?* Any alcoholic or addict, I thought to myself. I challenged his skepticism, but in the end I left feeling sad that this kind and brilliant man, a priest no less, had never been conscious enough of sin to find it miserable—not because I wanted him to suffer, but because I couldn't imagine how a person might have hope in Christ's resurrection if he had not first felt the violence of spiritual death or powerlessness in the face of temptation or the misery of seeing one's own sin in light of Christ's heart-piercing beauty. How could a person help but wail then?

•

Years later, the birth of my first son was going terribly wrong. I was in extraordinary pain. Unthinkable pain. The nurses seemed confused. *She's only dilated to a 4*, one said. It wasn't time for pain yet. But I was pale and shaking and hollowed out from agony. I moaned like a dying cow with each contraction and vomited into a plastic sack my husband held for me.

After the epidural was administered, I collapsed onto the hospital bed, exhausted and sweaty and euphoric. A nurse looked at me and smiled. Then she softly explained that women who were in a lot of pain when they received the epidural hardly felt the long needle entering their spine. They were just grateful and then blissed out in the absence of pain. But when women were not in pain, the epidural hurt, and they often complained (which was, in fact, my experience during labor with my second son). I think it's this way with sin. The more pain we're in, the less we mind the medicine.

•

I didn't like the meetings in McMinnville at first. The Eugene meetings had been full of sullen young people with lots of tattoos, who smoked cigarettes and were generally cooler than me. But in McMinnville, the crowd was different. Lots of older people, lots of poverty, lots of folks saying things like, *Sometimes life is just a big shit sandwich that you gotta choke down, and sometimes that shit tastes bad. Diarrhea bad.*

Back in Eugene, a woman had told me that when I didn't want to go to meetings, I should just take my feet. *The mind will follow*, she'd said. The more I thought about that idea, the more radical it seemed to me. Looking back, I saw how convinced I'd been that the mind should lead. First I think something is a good idea; then I do it. But I was learning the deep fallibility of my mind, how often it said one thing in the morning and another a night, and how unconscious I was of the incongruence between my many contradictory convictions. But what that woman back in Eugene said worked. Even when I could think of ten very good reasons to stay home and read a book or go out for a run, I took my feet to the recovery meeting. And for the most part, miraculously, my mind did follow.

It wasn't long before I began to hear the rough wisdom in what those McMinnville folks said. Soon, I started to look forward to meetings again. Even when little, brain-damaged, mean-faced Kofi drawled on about how he used to suck a glass dick (which I later learned meant a meth pipe), it seemed that jewels fell from his mouth. God, I am sure, was in that room, gently urging us toward love and humility, and so it was often he who spoke from the mouths of those who believed and those who didn't.

I began to learn another thing: God does not demand as much from us as we think, only that we take a step toward him. That's all.

The people I had judged, and with whom I was sure I had nothing in common, suddenly became my friends. Some of us met in coffee shops. Some of us went backpacking together. There were conventions and dances and dinners. And the strangeness of our little society filled me with joy. All the things that normally separate people (money, class, education, race, politics) melted in the face of this one urgent need—to stay sober. We were all on our knees, broken by the same thing, hungry for the same thing, restored by the same simple process of surrender.

In one recovery book it's said that people recovering from addiction are like survivors of a shipwreck. For a brief moment, everyone embraces and weeps and kisses one another's tears. But incredibly, I found people in those rooms with twenty or more years of sobriety who seemed to have dilated that moment to cover their lives. Because they came to meetings and heard again and again the story of their escape, they did not forget their brush with death—whether spiritual or physical. They were grateful, ready to help the next person escape the belly of the whale, or they were the belly of the whale.

•

That's one thing I've never understood about the book of Jonah. He says, *Throw me into the sea*, and the sailors toss him overboard. It's an act of honesty or confession. *It's me. I did it.* Then he is drowning. It seems as if drowning is death, but drowning is what he was doing the minute he boarded the ship. In the sea, the death that was already present is manifest. As he descends, his lungs are squeezed and his eyes start rolling back. Then the great fish is sent by God to swallow him, and the fish does swallow him, and after that, he is in darkness, being digested by an enormous underwater creature. And so there are two kinds of death—death that is an abyss, a death that leads only to death, and another death that might feel just as dark but leads to life. I wonder if Jonah knew the difference. Was he glad to be eaten? Sometimes "the belly of the whale" means something like "the worst possible situation," and sometimes it means "God has rescued you." Recovery meetings are like that, I think. Before, I was drowning, but I did not die. Instead, God sent me a great fish, and when I walked into the rooms of recovery, I was eaten.

•

I was one year sober when I went on a date with my Starbucks boss. Sanity returns slowly for some, it turns out. He was nice enough but not for me. I bowed out after the second date. As might have been predicted by anyone but me, my job there did not last long afterward. In a fit of anger, he sent me home one afternoon, and I decided not to go back.

Instead, a week later, I walked into a temp agency and put in my application. For a while, I did some filing work in a law office. Then, I went to an organic soda production plant, where I knelt on a little, wobbling, wooden board to pick broken glass off a conveyor belt. Bottles filled with carbonation often explode during temperature shifts, so it was my job to pick the glass off the belt without knocking any of the other bottles over. The only problem was, sometimes the bottles would explode very near to my face. They gave me plastic protective glasses, but they steamed up so badly that I couldn't see and would have to take them off to find shards of glass. It was like having a minefield roll under me. After a week, I handed back the glasses and said that eight dollars an hour was not enough to risk my sight. As I walked out, I saw them handing the glasses to a young Mexican kid, who hesitated before putting them around his head.

There were other jobs, mean jobs and fun jobs. Once I worked for two months at a flower farm, harvesting lavender. I loved sawing at the base of lavender bushes, one hand tightly gripping a fistful of stems, bees swarming my face in the hot sun. The smell was enough. And the view of that vast field of purple and then beyond, the gray and green hills and the rolling clouds. During lunch, we sat under big trees. The Mexican workers took off their sweat-soaked long shirts and hats in the shade, and we ate our sandwiches and oranges and drank water, and then I had a cigarette. There were children working alongside their parents, and sometimes they tried to teach me Spanish, laughing when I mispronounced words. But their laughter was kind, and all together we kept up a kind of rhythm, up and down the rows, sawing with rusted, crescent-moon saws, the women sometimes singing.

In those days, I prayed on my way to work. *God, I offer myself to thee, to build with me and to do with me as thou wilt. Relieve me of the bondage of self, that I may better do thy will. Take away my difficulties, that victory over them may bear witness to those I would help—of thy power, thy love, and thy way of life. May I do thy will always.*

I prayed because I did not want to work. Because I did not know how to. Because my back hurt. Because I was afraid of being fired again. The prayer worked a kind of magic over me, lifting me out of fear and setting me into the day like a fried egg on toast. The bipolar madness of both loathing and aspiring to work vanished, as I was reminded that my only job was to do the next right thing. *What's God's will for you for the next five minutes?* I'd ask myself.

More often than not, when I prayed, my work became easier. I noticed grasshoppers bounding around my feet and the tall spread of branches and the satisfaction of ache and sweat. The work felt honest, and under the high blue sky, I felt something like happiness.

•

On Saturdays I went over to my parents' house and mowed the lawn. Inevitably, at some point during the mowing, my dad would come out in sandals and socks, and he'd offer a comment about the weather or the heaviness of the grass or the efficiency of the lawn mower. I did not ruin the moment by telling him that I loved him, though I did love him and knew he loved me too.

Dad was softer in those days. The cold and refusing wall in him had started to melt, so that I could give him a kiss on the cheek, and he would smile and then sweetly, awkwardly put his whiskers against my cheek in return and then pat me on the back and walk away, still smiling.

In the late afternoon, we sometimes rode our bikes out of McMinnville into the rolling hills, where rich people kept vineyards, and the honey of ripe fruit filled the air, and the slant sun shot out its amber blankets over the dead grass and the wildflowers. I always rode behind him and watched his impossibly pale and wide calves flex as he peddled up hills and sprinted the flats. I was instinctively comforted by his strength. If I saw a speed sign that read thirty-five miles per hour, I yelled up to my dad, *Hey! You better slow down!* and he always chuckled because he liked jokes like that.

Every once in a while, I'd ask him something about Plato or Heidegger. And sometimes, if the wind was favorable and the ride wasn't too hard, he would entertain the question. He liked to talk that way, both our eyes fixed on the road, the world rushing past. And we would be amazed at butterflies and hawks together and our legs burned, and we offered one another manly compliments. Our speech was monotone. No superlatives were admitted. *Saw that push on the last hill*, I might say, and then he might say back, *Well it's better at the top*.

We turned around at mile 14, when our road met a highway running perpendicular to it. But before we started home, we got off our bikes and walked around in the shade of a few great oaks and looked at sculptures in a garden outside the art gallery there. Nearby, there was a wine shop and another little store that sold blown glass. I remember watching my gray-bearded and bespectacled dad in his clip-clopping bike shoes, and his orange, tight-fitting riding outfit, and his unbuckled helmet still on his head, as he bent over an iron figure of a frog as though he were trying to figure it out. When he straightened, he grunted as though he'd solved the mystery.

# CHAPTER 13

•

After the lavender fields and the soda factory, there was an orthodontics plant, where I spent eight hours a day listening to audiobooks as I used tweezers to arrange tiny metal brackets on a laminated sheet. Nine hundred brackets per sheet. Many sheets a day. And then, one day, the temp agency called and offered me a job at a monastery.

I couldn't believe my good luck. It was a men's Brigittine monastery just outside of Amity. Most monastic communities have some kind of trade that brings in money. The monks of New Skete raise and train beautiful German shepherds. One dog goes for about ten thousand dollars. The nuns at the same monastery make cheesecake. There are Trappists who make jams. Benedictines who make beer. Orthodox monasteries often make prayer ropes and sell hand-painted icons. But the Brigittines of Amity make fudge and chocolate truffles, and I was going to help them.

The first day, I drove my 1986 Volvo sedan down Highway 18, then turned onto a little, winding country road with vast orchards to either side, and then eventually onto a gravel road. The road ended at the monastery, a squat, brown series of buildings tucked in among tall, leafy trees.

A cheerful Filipino monk came out to greet me. Morning prayer would be starting soon, he said, so we didn't have much time. He quickly escorted me to the small production facility at the rear of the main building. Inside, I saw huge metal mixing vats, into which a middle-aged man, clearly not a monk, was dumping marshmallow fluff and butter. There were tens of high trolleys with racks of fudge already cooling and a commercial dishwashing setup and conveyor belts, and everything gleamed of chrome and copper and machines chirred rhythmically, almost drowning out the quiet voice of the monk who was explaining the machinery to me.

Further back, in the next room, I found a machine that put cellophane wrapping over boxes, and that is where I was told to wait.

The bells summoning monks to prayer sounded faintly against the din of work. The monk gave me one final smile and scurried off.

•

It was a small monastery, I soon learned. Only twelve or so monks lived there at any given time, many of whom were elderly and frail. The order of Saint Brigit is not a major order. There are only about eight hundred members worldwide, and of them the only men's Brigittine monastery was the one in which I stood. So, those twelve men were it: the monk who stayed in bed all day and made YouTube videos of himself doing facial exercises; the monk who had dementia and had to be fed pudding with a spoon; the four or five young Filipino men who were lively and gentle and ready to laugh; and five others.

The monastery was a little noble and a little sad. Soon, the old guard would die off, and who would replace them? I imagined the young monks twenty years down the line, no longer young, alone in the large building, their footsteps echoing too loudly.

They were an island and the sea was rising, and soon even the trees would be covered. But it seemed to me unlikely that the younger monks would leave. Someday there would be three, and then two, and then one. And all the while they would kneel in the dark chapel and sing the psalms and look out across the empty space to their crucified Lord. And though that image was hard and mean in one sense, in another I imagined the persistence of their joy, the joy of the crucified and raised—joy unknown to the rest of us who ask, again and again, *What makes me happy?*

The abbot once told me that sometimes Brigittine sisters from a convent in Mexico traveled up to visit them. And when they did, the whole monastery feasted. They ate fatty meat and lit fireworks at night and had small glasses of port in the evening. And the sisters brought the gift of their boisterous laughter. The nuns especially loved, he told me, to take fishing poles down to the small pond behind the monastery and sit out in the sun all day under wide-brimmed hats, catching fish and sucking on lollipops and chatting with their old monk friends.

•

That first day I waited next to the wrapping machine until a man in his fifties, wearing the typical gray robe with red cross on the breast, came shuffling from the main house toward me. His head was bowed as he walked, but he glanced up briefly when he was near me and then bowed his head again and instructed me to follow him.

He shuffled (I would soon learn that Brother Martin only ever shuffled, there was no other mode of movement for him) toward a small closet-sized room. Standing close together in the cramped room, he let me know that this was the truffle room. I looked around. There was a deep counter and behind us, high on the wall, a shelf stacked with boxes. But there was no window. The only light came from a gently humming yellow bulb fixed to the ceiling.

The next day, we began to work together, side by side, except when Brother Martin went to prayer or when he needed a nap. He showed me the manual machine we used to squeeze great blocks of truffle filling into little inch-long cylinders. Pink cherry, chocolate, pale amaretto. Then we rolled the cylinders of paste between our palms to make little balls; then we put the balls onto trays and eventually brought them over to a large conveyor belt that coated them in chocolate.

We spent a lot of time in silence, but sometimes Brother Martin told me about himself. He'd grown up in New Mexico and knew early on that he wanted to be a monk. But his priest told him to wait until he was thirty. *No one knows anything until he is thirty*, he'd said. Though he worked for some time at a bank, his sense of vocation never wavered. Even when he suffered a brain-damaging heat stroke (something I was told by one of the staff), and his personality changed, he did not forget the desire to pray, to spend his whole life in prayer. *That's how I ended up here,* he said. I nodded, though I still had a lot of questions.

He wore glasses and was always serious and did not care for jokes, though he made them without knowing it. Once, we were talking about the Catholic Church when he said, apropos of nothing, *Those Buddhists. Yeess, you have to be careful of Buddhists. Mm-hmm. They love gooold.* (That's how he spoke, with a lisp and elongated vowels and *s*'s.) *Yeess, they are very rich, the Buddhistss.* To which I asked, *Aren't Catholics also rich?* He shook his head as though I were stupid. *See my shoess? They are thirteen yearss old. I like these shoess. They're broown.*

The topic having been exhausted in his mind, we resumed our silent pressing and rolling.

Another time, I asked Brother Martin, *If you could pick one superpower, what would you choose?* He closed his eyes thoughtfully. When he opened them, he said, *I would like to have Xsss-raaay vision.* He started rolling truffle balls again. *Why?* I asked. He pointed to the boxes stacked on a high shelf behind us and said with no small amount of frustration, *Those boxxesss! I can never tell what'ss in them. Are they brooown cups? Or whiiiite cups? If I haaad Xx-ray vision I could pick the riiight boxx every tiiiime.* The bells started to chime as he finished his thought. He dropped the pink ball he'd been working on, and, with a tenderness I'll never forget, he said, *Noon prayer!* And his face shone with real joy, and he turned and shuffled out the door.

•

After the first day, I rode my bike the twelve miles to work. It was spring and then summer. The trees leafed out, and the mottled sky raised its bodies of cloud and sent them, gray wisp and fog, across the hilltops in soft morning light. There were birds, as there almost always are, ospreys and sparrows and chickadees. My thighs whimpered as I pushed the bike forward, and the dust rose in the air, catching light. Sometimes, I stopped along the way by a copse of trees or a fence and got off my bike and stared out over a field of alfalfa, watching the wind rake it back and forth.

Many days, I was late to work, partly because I didn't know how not to be. If someone else had been there, someone else's eyes on the scene, I wouldn't have felt so *responsible*. But there was no one else standing by the road as the field opened out: the arc of bird flight, the stubble of shorn grass, the mellow yielding of tree line to sky. How perfect the giant steel wheel seemed to me propped up against an old barn. If anyone else had been there to see and translate and offer the world back to God, I could have peddled on. But each morning the scene was new and rare and demanded my attention.

The monks did not care too much about tardiness, but the foreman of the chocolate factory was not impressed. He did not like my sweaty, windblown appearance or the time I spent changing into a new shirt or the position of the minute hand, now showing fifteen minutes past the hour, when I finally headed to the truffle closet. And, of course, I knew I was wrong to waste the monks' money on my private, aesthetic reveries. It never occurred to me that I could leave earlier. What's a girl to do? It seemed to me that God was offering me a gift. There were words and music attached to those scenes, and though the meaning was never clear, the atrophied nerves of my heart began to sting.

•

I'd never entirely stopped writing poetry. Before getting sober, I would smoke a little weed or drink a few glasses of wine. *To get the juices flowing*, I said to myself. I'd read about Apollo and Dionysus in Nietzsche's *The Birth of Tragedy* and had a great theory worked out. Poetry was Dionysian. It came from the poet's ability to overcome the Apollonian instinct for reason and embraced the world in all its primordial mystery. To quiet the anxious, critical, Apollonian voice in my head, I needed a sedative. Just a few drinks. Maybe two drinks and a single hit off my tiny pipe.

There were other artists who backed up my theory—not, maybe, the Nietzschean part, but the intoxication part, definitely. Dylan Thomas and Truman Capote, Faulkner, Hemingway, Cheever. There were women, too: Ann Sexton, Elizabeth Bishop, Patricia Highsmith.

But instead of tapping into primordial mystery, I wrote frenetic poems about squirrels, which I thought were brilliant at the time of writing. Only after drinking coffee and having a cigarette the next morning did I discover that my poems were stupid.

After getting sober, I was delighted to see that my writing improved. I read a lot of Charles Wright and Gerard Manley Hopkins in those days. I loved the way they *saw*. That seemed the whole thing to me, seeing. Simone Weil once wrote that attention is a form of prayer, and I believed these two poets were saints of attention. I'd always been sensitive to beauty in the world, but now that the chemical veil had started to lift, I began to notice the sound of words that seemed to just kind of erupt out of little scenes. An alleyway. An incandescent bug. The world was singing. Sorrowful songs and plaintive songs, defiant songs and awe-filled. It was not prayer because it felt entirely receptive, but it shared with prayer that sense of communion and radiance.

My poems were still pretty bad. But I entered two of them into a tiny, local poetry contest and won both first and second prize. At the award ceremony, half the audience was made up of my sober friends, many of whom had never read a poem in their lives. But they loved me, and it didn't matter that my poems were a little embarrassing or that my friends weren't literary people who wore flowy scarves or smart-looking glasses. There was Kofi and a former Air Force pilot; a stay-at-home mom; a giant, kind, schizophrenic man; a nurse; a man in his forties who'd just started at the local community college; and many others. Between poems, I looked up and saw their beaming faces. Afterward, they had a little party for me and a cake. It is one of my happiest memories.

A professor of fiction at my alma mater somehow read those two poems and wrote me a Facebook message saying, among other things, *When are you going to get that MFA?* It was all the encouragement I needed.

# 14

# Riverside, California

*The day when God is absent, when He is silent—that is the beginning of prayer.*

Anthony Bloom, *Beginning to Pray*

I applied to some of the best schools for creative writing because, I don't know, why not? I had no idea how unprepared I was. Iowa, Virginia, the University of Texas at Austin. Understandably, they rejected me. But I did get into the University of California, Riverside (UCR), which I applied to only because one of my best sober friends had a brother doing a PhD in philosophy there.

I knew nothing about Riverside or the writing program. But I loaded up my blue Volvo with all my worldly belongings, kissed my parents goodbye, and drove south. I made the drive in one long, sixteen-hour go. It was early September, a hot month in what was a very hot year. My Volvo didn't have AC or radio, so I kept the windows down and sang loudly into the wind as the landscape morphed from lush evergreen to high desert. The blacktop snaked the Klamath Mountains, then past Mount Shasta, her snowcap glistening in thin air, and then down into the hot, dry valley of central California. I passed fields filled with what seemed like millions of cows all pressed together in mud and poo. Feed lots, I think. It was horrible to see. There might have been dead cows pressed into the shit, and you'd never know. The fetid smell was so overwhelming I was forced to choose between rolling up my widows so that my car became a steel furnace or suffering the pong. I chose the pong. Windows down, I thought of all the microscopic flecks of cow turd hurtling through my window and up my nose. But it was still preferable to the heat.

Once the sun dipped out, the smell faded and the vast open sky lifted her skirt to show the beauty she'd been hiding. A field of bright, ancient starlight. I felt a little sorry for the photons that entered my pupils then. After flying through the depths of space, past supernovas and icy planets, after the vast, dark emptiness of space they defiantly illuminated, a journey of perhaps thousands or millions of years, they landed in my Volvo, which still carried the ripe smell of animal waste.

But then I remembered that Christ was into that sort of thing. Light landing in stables, which probably also smelled slightly of poo. And I was happier to receive the gift—oceanic beauty, subatomic humility, the weird glory of a God I loved and could not understand.

On the way down, the rhythm of tire thumping and wind got a little poem going in my head. I pulled over and wrote down a few lines from time to time. The poem and the stars and my overtired mind together seemed to confirm the goodness of my trajectory. I felt that God himself had laid his hand on me. *Write it*, he seemed to say.

•

I wasn't one of those kids who grew up wanting to be a writer. Under the influence of my dad, I thought of the arts as soft and feminine and frilly. I'd wanted to be hard—a hard soldier or a hard, disciplined thinker. Philosophy fit the bill. So did mountain climbing and soldiering, whereas poetry seemed like existential ornamentation, weakly dependent on feeling and intuition.

But poetry had come to me in the darkest moments of my life as a language of hope. When the rigors of self-mastery bellied up, poetry arrived like a raft. Against despair, it lifted me, tilting my head, and there was the sky always breathing and new, the light-blurring clouds and their incomprehensible song.

I gravitated toward poets who wrote in a mode of salvific seeing. Eliot and his midwinter spring; Auden and his sobbing, spinning world; Hopkins's dappled things; Levertov's mountain; Wright's backyard; Glück's iris; Dickinson's fly. They came for me, somehow against my will, and laid a claim on me. I didn't think writing poetry was a sign of intellectual sophistication. It was about reality and survival. It was still hard. Or I came to it with a hardness in me, making demands of language. *Prove yourself,* I felt myself saying, again and again.

•

I pulled up to a house in Moreno Valley, a suburb of Riverside. There was a little street lined with palm trees and cacti and sun-pummeled rock. To the left, the road seemed to lead straight into the Box Spring Mountains, which stood only half proud above our suburban strip. They looked like transplants from Mars—dry and ferrous. I unpacked my stuff from the Volvo and started to carry it inside. That's when I met the wonderful, anxious, self-doubting fiction writer who was to be my roommate. He greeted me at the front door. Tall and thin and wearing a little beanie and round glasses, Kevin reminded me of Waldo, and I liked him instantly.

Kevin and I had met in a Facebook group for MFA students at UCR and agreed to be roommates. I found the house online. He approved. Neither of us had been there before we signed the rental agreement. Now I saw that it was weirdly large. We wouldn't be able to furnish it, but the rent was cheap, so who cared?

Kevin was as surprised to find himself in grad school as I was. He came from a poor family in northern Indiana. He was a skinny-jeans skater, who suffered terribly from impostor syndrome. Some nights he got drunk and sad. Other times he sat at his desk for long hours, typing and deleting and hating himself the whole time, or at least that's how it seemed to me. But he was also one the funniest people I had ever met, and I have a terrible affection for self-conscious people, having been one for so long, so that after a little while I came to love him with a pure, innocent love.

•

The poetry program at UCR was under the ostensible leadership of California's poet laureate. He had us coloring on construction paper and doing yoga in class and other, equally "zany" and "fun" activities. I did not do a great job of hiding my disdain. *Don't edit your poems!* he once advised. *I wrote a whole book of poems while waiting for a haircut. I never edited it.* Later, *Maybe you could put feathers on the cover. Think about how you can mix and blend and liquefy and launch different media. Why does a poetry book need to be a rectangle?* I wanted to shoot myself.

There were good poets who taught there, too. They were serious about their work and made serious demands of us, but most were on their way out. I took one class from each of them before they left and pressed what oil I could from their instruction and read the new poets they introduced and understood from them, at least, how little I knew about poetry. Maybe that's a good reason to get an MFA.

But most of the time I was frustrated. I needed language to do more than it was being asked to do in workshops. We spent a lot of time talking about fresh and novel language, and so a person might substitute the word "sulfur" for "yellow" just because it was a stranger word and not because the poem demanded it. I recoiled from novelty for its own sake. If poetry was going to keep me alive, as it had, it needed to be concerned with reality.

Besides, I thought, the further a person presses into experience, the more strange it reveals itself to be. It becomes more particular, less abstract. Colors more vivid or less, but almost never matching up with the symbolic idea I might have been carrying around. I wanted poetry disciplined in the art of sinking its teeth into the dog bone of life. It seemed to me that language that takes its starting place in the real is always fresh, always startling because it's a living language.

My hunger for this kind of poetry made me a poor workshop participant. I had a violent need that manifested in dismissive critiques of what I thought of as play poetry or stupid poetry or vain poetry. I'm sure I seemed stuck up, though I don't think anyone was overly offended because it's not like I was writing great poems. But I wasn't stuck up, or not only stuck up. I was desperate.

•

There was a young woman there. A brilliant fiction writer. I loved her and envied her. Where I was raw and coarse and full of furious impulse, she was refined, reserved, and technically masterful. She was the queen of our cohort, or at least I thought so, though I don't think she knew it. We eyed each other warily. But we were also friends, real friends sometimes.

Once, I went over to her house for dinner and watched as she cut individual leaves of spinach into slivers for a salad. The cutting was slow because she kept pausing to speak. I'd never in my life cut a leaf of spinach. When I wanted a salad, I grabbed a fistful of leaves out of the bag and plopped them in a bowl, and that was that.

Somehow we got on the subject of dads. Hers lived in Arizona. She did his voice sort of drawling and stupid and tough. She laughed as she told me about the time he'd cut off his finger with a table saw and then taped it back on, wrapped a towel around it, and kept working. Then I told her about the time my dad was sick and studying at the library. His fever rose and he started groaning, but didn't leave his books until his intestines literally exploded. He got up from the desk then and made it to the stairs. A janitor found him crumpled at the bottom of the stairwell and called an ambulance. We laughed. And then I said that sometimes I thought about my dad dying. She nodded, as though it were a familiar topic.

*When he dies, I'll run down the street naked and screaming*, she said.

*Yeah, I sort of imagine going insane and tearing out my hair.*

*It won't happen.* She shook her head. *Can't.*

•

I went to recovery meetings in Riverside and made friends with women who weren't in grad school, some who hadn't graduated from high school. But they were bright and genuine and at home in themselves—sort of the opposite of most writers. After class, I went over to their houses and forgot about writing. We smoked and laughed and talked about boys and hockey and God.

But at night I picked up my keys and made a fist with the metal poking out between my fingers, like claws. And I ran the dark and orange-lit streets into Riverside, into the rough part of town, methtown. As I ran, I hoped someone would try to jump me. I imagined it over and over again. Keys entering the eye socket, the blood. What would I bite? How would it feel? Did I want to hurt or be hurt? I didn't know.

I didn't understand why I thought that way, except that it was loosely connected to the Army. When I mentioned those violent thoughts to other sober women, they weren't surprised, which surprised me. They nodded, as though they had the same dream. And they told me about what men had done, and the barely conscious rage they felt.

Once, Tom Lutz declared to our nonfiction class, *What's wrong with your writing is what's wrong with you*. It's one of the few things from that time I remember to this day. I think it's true. In those days, I had a hard time closing the gap between what I thought I wanted to write and what I actually wrote. My poems were almost always circling something they couldn't land on. There was a hole in the middle of them, as if I were keeping something at arm's length.

•

Shortly before classes ended in spring, I signed up for a wildland firefighting course. I'm not sure why, except maybe I needed the earth again, hands in the dirt, sweating. Real work. In any case, the California Conservation Corps (CCC) had a program for veterans. You sign up with them for a month-long summer program, and they train you to be a wildland firefighter. If things go well, you might get assigned to a BLM or Forest Service crew.

So after the first year of the MFA was done and all my papers were turned in, I packed my giant, purple backpacking backpack with clothes and books and got on a train for Tahoe.

•

Tahoe sits 6,225 feet above sea level. The air is fine and thin and filled with the smell of sunburned sap. Tall pines and white fir cover the hills that rise steeply from Lake Tahoe's shore. Long, pale wands of lupine line the road, and yellow cress and arrowroot and purple thistles.

The Tahoe CCC was made up of a few white barracks and a headquarters building off Apache Avenue. I lugged my backpack off the bus and stood outside the headquarters with the other new kids. They were young, much younger than me. I was twenty-nine that summer, and they seemed to have just graduated from high school. The boys tried to look serious and tough. Maybe I also wanted to seem tough, so I stood apart at first, waiting for something to happen.

Soon we were given uniforms. Soon we stood in formation. Soon we were told to iron those uniforms and sew badges into them. And soon, without realizing it, or only half realizing it, I was back in the Army. And the boys around me, the rough boys from rough parts of California, the ones who drank a lot and who were hopped up on hormones and inexperience, were indistinguishable from the boys of Darmstadt or San Antonio.

I didn't like that part—the familiar, incestuous feel of barracks life. Boys spreading gross rumors about any woman out of earshot. But during the day, we worked high up in the hills, overlooking the calm, bright eye of the lake below. We trudged pathless routes to sections of forest that needed thinning and were taught how to use a chain saw to fell trees. There was an old man who showed us how to inspect a tree, its lean, the surrounding limbs and cables that could snag a falling tree midair. Inspection complete, a path of retreat cleared, the old man yanked the saw's starter cord, and the motor roared to life. I watched its razor teeth moving so fast they were invisible as they sank into tree flesh. Fine curls of pale wood flying to the east and the west. The smell of gasoline and oil and dust. Then a back cut, a pounded wedge, a yell to warn people nearby of the incredible weight falling from the sky.

We stomped around in the woods like that felling trees, bucking and limbing them, carrying heavy tree rounds and limbs to burn piles, cutting through manzanita, a bush that quickly became famous among us as a pernicious and evil plant. Because manzanita is invasive, it dominates the understory. Its wood is hard, but because it's a bush, it gives under the weight of the saw and resists cutting.

During lunch we sat in the open air. We were dirt smeared and sweat soaked and the sun glittered below us on the lake's open palm. And there were wildflowers between my legs as I sat on a hill and opened my lunch sack and ate my sandwich. The cheese was fatty, and the heat was like butter, and the whole world seemed to me then like a feast.

•

Many weekends, my new friends went to Stateline, a little blip of a town built around resorts and casinos on the California-Nevada border. I went with them and watched as they drank in hotel bars and gambled at casinos.

I used to say that I didn't know why I went with them. But the truth is I do know. I wanted a little vicarious taste. I got an adrenaline bump when I got into the cab with them but kept secret, especially from myself, how much I still wanted the glowing, golden feel of drunkenness—how light seemed to get bigger and softer all at once—and the expansive, floating sense that all was well and easy and fun. *Just a little taste*, I did not allow myself to say to myself.

Then one Friday night, I was sitting at a hotel bar by myself while everyone else was dancing or playing poker, and there were go-go dancers with dead eyes bopping up and down in high boots behind me. When the bartender came by to see if I wanted a Diet Coke refill, I ordered two shots of tequila. Not one. I wasn't going to kid myself. I'd been sober just over two years. No longer. The shots went down like freedom and remorse all mixed together. Then I ordered two more.

The next morning, I woke and resolved that I wouldn't let it happen again. I'd relapsed before but never after such a long stretch of sobriety. I was ashamed, though nothing terrible had happened. At some point, I'd stumbled out of the hotel and found a cab and didn't puke on the way home.

So, I started going to meetings in town after work. I went to one on Sunday and kept going every day after work. There was a man about my age at those meetings. He was deafeningly handsome, and I felt his beautiful eyes on me when I raised my hand to admit that I'd had a drink after two years sober. He talked to me after the meeting, and I suddenly found that I wanted desperately to stay sober. *I'm one of the sane ones*, I wanted to say to him.

But that Thursday was the Fourth of July. We didn't work that day. Instead, I woke up early and went for a run through the meadows and came back to my barracks room and showered and ate a good breakfast. In the chow hall everyone was talking about their plans for the evening. When they invited me to go along, I shook my head. I was sober again, and I wanted to stay that way.

But one of the things that a lot of people don't understand about alcoholics, or at least alcoholics like me, is that the part of myself that I depend on to make good choices, the moral or sane part, malfunctions if I've had a drink recently. It's as though when I'm sober, there is a golden cord that connects me to God. That cord transmits an affection for truth and goodness and peace and gives me a subtle power to pursue those things. But once a drink hits my bloodstream, the cord is cut, the connection scrambled. It's not God who does the scrambling. It's the other one. "The disease," many of us call it. But I know it by another name, too.

I meant to stay sober. I wanted to. But by two in the afternoon, I'd agreed to climb a mountain with my friends to watch the fireworks. I knew they would be drinking, but I convinced myself I would just sit on a rock and watch the sunset and the fireworks blaze and I would write little poems in my book and drink soda.

By four, I was at the grocery store buying snacks, and I watched my friend slide a bottle of vodka toward the cashier. I had carrots and strawberries and Diet Coke in my basket. *Be right back!* I called to my friend, and I ran to the wine aisle and, shaking, grabbed a cheap Pinot and ran back. Then, on second thought, I went back for another bottle. My head was full of the sound of blood as I handed the cashier my debit card. I couldn't hear anything outside of the whoosh, whoosh of adrenaline and the sound of the bottles clinking together in their plastic bag.

We did climb the mountain, and I think there were fireworks. But the rest of the night is a blur punctuated by brief glimpses of me chasing someone around the mountaintop, a huge fire, someone handing me a joint.

When I woke up, the sun was blistering my skin. I sat up, in terrible pain, and saw that I had fallen asleep on an anthill. Where were my pants? My mouth was dry. My eyes were dry. The mountaintop was empty except for one other guy. Was he waiting for me?

We hiked down in dehydrated silence.

•

It was less than a week between June 28, the day I picked up a drink, a day that had started out as a normal and happy day, and July 5, the day I hiked down a mountain in suicidal shame. I nearly lost my job at the CCC over that night, though I was never entirely sure what I'd done. But the worst part was the way the other kids looked at me. I had been a relatively stable person amid the sea of hormone-addled youth. But something had broken that night. They saw me as I was, I thought. The real Kate. Drunk Kate. And I wanted to die.

That's the disease. First a drink. Then the inability to control the drink. Then a broken mind, unable to see past despair. Then death.

One night I called Raphi. I was curled up under the sink in the bathroom. I didn't know what else to do. He was probably an alcoholic, too, and knew the gentle slope leading to hopelessness. But he didn't console me. *Call your sponsor*, he'd said. And shortly after, he hung up. I didn't want to call her. I knew what she would say, or thought I did, and I didn't want what she could offer. I'd tried all that and it hadn't worked. Nearly four years of doing step work and going to meetings and showing up after relapses and calling people and making friends, and what had it gotten me?

I was down, down. The world so small. Dark every way I looked. I wanted to end it. Without saying it out loud, I made up my mind. How else could I escape myself?

During the day I did my work and the trees were still running their sap and the lupines still leaned in the wind. But I was saying goodbye.

But I couldn't shake Raphi's voice saying over and over again, *Call your sponsor.* In the shower, I heard it. Watching a tree fall, I heard it. Eating fries, I heard it. The next morning, knowing that it would change nothing, I called her. Just to quiet the voice. Like I said, I knew what she would say. I knew what I would say. But I picked up the phone.

*Hello?*

*Hey Trina. How's it going?*

*Good, good. How's Tahoe?*

*Good.* Then I inhaled, teetering on the edge of something.

*I drank a few days ago.*

*Oh?*

*Yeah. And I'm not doing too good. I don't know, um . . . I don't, uh, know if. Never mind.*

*Kate?*

*Yeah.*

*Kate, how dark does it seem now?*

*Pretty dark.*

*Can you see the light from where you are?*

*No.*

*Okay. I'm going to say something my sponsor once told me. You don't have to believe me, but what I'm about to say is true. Even though it's dark, unbearably dark right now, and you can't see your way out, if you can stay sober today—Kate, are you listening?*

*Yeah.*

*If you can stay sober today, you will walk in the light again. I promise.*

I cried then. What could I say? She hadn't said what I thought she would. Or, she had, but somehow I'd been pierced.

•

There's no explanation for it. She hadn't said anything all that special. But I think some kind of angel bore the words from her mouth and planted them in my heart and gave them life so that I believed her when she said the light would come back. Trina told me to read a couple pages out of a book for alcoholics and pray each day. *Help*, I was supposed to say before getting out of bed and *thank you* before getting under the covers at night. So that's what I did.

I prayed when, after the CCC training was done, I was assigned to a notoriously tough Forest Service hand crew. *Help. Thank you.* And I prayed when one of the guys, drunk and fumbling, broke into my cabin room and put his hands under my covers. *Help.* I prayed in the mountains during a lighting storm, our metal tools waving around in the air above our heads. *Help.* I prayed on the fireline at night when trees exploded into flame with a power I didn't know trees possessed, God somehow in the fire—its torch and awful beauty—and in the cool damp of night air, down on the green side of a hill. *Thank you. Help*, I prayed when I turned on my headlamp to find a bag of Sun Chips in my backpack and saw that I was surrounded by scorpions. I whispered *thank you* when I tilted my head back and watched waves of red, glowing embers fly across the black sky. And when the other crew members grew suspicious of me because I didn't drink and because I listened to Edith Piaf and sometimes sat by myself reading *Anna Karenina*, I prayed.

When I left Tahoe to go back to school, I still prayed. But the light did not come back. Not then. For months, prayer felt like rocks in my mouth. Like I was knocking at the side of a mountain, asking it to open up. Stone and stone. *Help.*

## 15

# Riverside, California

*Why should she give her bounty to the dead? . . .*
*Shall she not find in comforts of the sun,*
*In pungent fruit and bright, green wings, or else*
*In any balm or beauty of the earth,*
*Things to be cherished like the thought of heaven?*

Wallace Stevens, "Sunday Morning"

Back in Riverside, the sun bore down like a great unblinking eye. Inland Empire sun is a meth addict, never sleeping, alert, pummeling the dry earth. And there were rattlesnakes under rocks and coyotes in the hills, and dry-feathered birds, and the plants were spiked.

Kevin and I moved out of the house in Moreno Valley into an apartment with our friend, a smart, wealthy kid from Houston. In the heat and dead air we lifted furniture out of a U-Haul and carried it up the steps. The two boys, thin-limbed and pale, were not pleased with the way I ran up and down the steps, carrying the heaviest items. But I'd spent the summer lugging heavy packs up mountains and working the earth with tools. It's work that makes couches light, and so, without meaning to, I shamed them.

I liked the look of my body in the mirror, so lithe and firm and capable. It was a body good for work. But back in the city, back in the world of cars and strip malls and school, my body lost its purpose.

I felt that I was a head borne around by a meat chariot. At school, the meat chariot could be beautiful or ugly but was not, in and of itself, important. The principal thing was the mind.

For a while, I tried to keep the feeling of physical competence alive. I went for long hikes in the Box Spring Mountains, ran a half-marathon, jogged up steep desert hills, but there was no work to do. Nothing needed hauling or sawing or digging. I didn't need to be strong for anyone but myself.

Classes started back up again. And there I was, a brain looking through the eyes, using the hands to amplify a thought the brain came up with, crossing and uncrossing the legs to signal whatever it was I wanted to sign. My sense of self retracted up into the cranium.

•

It wasn't until I was in an MFA program that I noticed the *look* of female writers, especially poets. Think Emily Dickenson, Sylvia Plath, Christina Rossetti, Anna Akhmatova, Louise Glück, Anne Carson. Think dark eyes and hair, pale skin, and limbs so thin they could almost float off. That's the look: about to drift away. A look that accentuates the head and the eyes because that's the site of poetic vision. The body should be small and light, expressing ambivalence about its own existence.

•

In the weeks before classes started, I went to a lot of recovery meetings and was happy to be with my sober friends. I told them what had happened in Tahoe, and they told me how glad they were I'd made it back.

But after the meetings and sometimes before, I would stop at a frozen yogurt shop and make a giant cup filled with sugar-yogurt and topped with whatever I liked: gummy bears and sprinkles, graham crackers and M&M's, whipped cream. And I would sit in one of the plastic chairs and, not looking at anyone, lift massive spoonfuls into my mouth. Then I would throw my cup away and go to the bathroom. When I emerged, I was sweating a bit and my face was red and my eyes were bloodshot, and I hurried out the door.

I started carrying a toothbrush and toothpaste in my purse.

•

Back in McMinnville, I'd been sober from alcohol but not from everything else. After work, in the evenings, I often walked from my apartment over to the grocery store, crossing the parking lot in the dark. And then, under the buzz of fluorescent light, I power walked up and down the aisles, dropping sweet foods into my basket. I knew which foods were easy to get up and which got stuck. I wanted the forbidden foods, the foods no woman in daylight would be seen eating in the quantities she desired: ice cream and sweet cereal and Little Debbie cakes.

Sometimes, as I was preparing to leave the house, a voice would come: *You don't have to*. It was such a quiet voice, not at all forceful. And so, as I walked across the parking lot in the dark, my mind split in two. One part hearing and longing to comply with the voice, *You can stop. The night is full of stars*. The other already high on dopamine, a juggernaut of desire.

Back in my apartment, I drew the blinds and set the food down in a little circle around me and spent hours half watching Netflix while I ate. There was no voice then. Every twenty or so minutes I paused the show and got up from my chair to throw up. In a single night I might vomit seven or eight times. I hated myself and loved the numb of it all and felt an acute and painful distance from God. But at least I felt something about God—there, on the other side of a great distance and a glass wall, was the one I loved. And that seemed preferable to the other, which was not having any consciousness of him at all.

•

In those days, I liked to arrange my books on my coffee table before going to bed. If I were to die, I wanted people to see that I'd been reading Kierkegaard. It's such a stupid thought that I want to laugh now, only it's too sad. I really believed that if I died in the night from puking up Captain Crunch, my parents would be consoled by my reading list. I couldn't imagine their grief or anger and instead saw only the horror of being misunderstood in the end. So, night after night, I arranged my death mask and went to bed.

•

Once, I went to the VA hospital because my heart wasn't working right. Too slow. Thirty-six beats a minute. Thirty-five. I kept wobbling between consciousness and blackout. I was honest with the doctors about the eating disorder. *Your heart will sort itself out if your electrolytes are balanced. That can't happen as long as you're actively bulimic*, the doctor said. But I couldn't hear it. Instead, I started adding electrolyte powder to my water.

•

In Riverside, one of my sober friends called to invite me over. I'd just thrown up and was washing my hands when she called. I said I couldn't come. I was sick, I said. *Sick?* She seemed to know the truth.

*Come over anyway*, she said.

*But I won't talk. I'm . . . numb.*

*Come anyway*, she insisted.

That evening I told her the whole truth while we sat in her backyard. And when other people came over I was still kind of high and far away. But the shame had melted off, and it felt unreasonably good to be there with them in the middle of my sin. Not in my little dark room.

•

I'm not sure what my roommates thought about my secretive evenings. Maybe they didn't notice. It wasn't uncommon for me to retreat to my room when they had people over to drink. Sometimes, I came out in my jammies and asked them to smoke weed on the balcony so I wouldn't have to smell it. I knew how lame I sounded but didn't care. I didn't want any of it around me anymore.

Things escalated from frozen yogurt to vending machine binges to whole grocery baskets. Soon, classes would start. I was supposed to teach a poetry class, and I was at war. *Help.* I prayed. I was sober and not sober, and the light was still a long way off.

It was around that time that I realized what I had to do. Trina finally suggested that if I wanted to stay sober, I'd have to deal with the other stuff, too. The eating disorder kept me spiritually ill, cut off from God. She told me to pray an old recovery prayer: *My Creator, I am now willing that you should have all of me. Please remove from me every single defect of character that stands in the way of my usefulness to you and my fellows. Grant me strength, as I go out from here, to do your bidding.* So I prayed, even though I did not believe that anything—not God or psychiatry or willpower—could heal that deep pit of hunger. It was a fathomless mystery to me, as permanent and powerful as the sea.

But a few weeks later, I was sitting in my car outside of an eating-disorder treatment program. I knew the odds. Eating disorders have the highest mortality rate among psychiatric conditions, and only a very few afflicted recover. But alcoholism had prepared me. Despite the fact that I considered myself an expert in nutrition and exercise, I'd need to surrender to their program, no matter how stupid it seemed to me. *Become teachable* is how Trina put it. I couldn't heal myself. If I'd been able to, I would have already.

It was an ordinary parking lot, just like any other parking lot in America. Ornamental shrubs at the base of a tan medical building. The palm trees waved in the wind. And there was a bougainvillea growing against the wall. But for me, that day, the parking lot was a battleground. I picked up my folder, filled with medical forms I'd filled out, shut the car door authoritatively and half marched toward the doors.

•

Sin is a word with a wide web of connotations. It's often seen in the legal sense of having broken the law. But that's not what I mean when I say that I sat in the middle of it. For the Orthodox, sin is understood in a medical, rather than judicial, sense. Sin as disease, as affliction. The distinction is important. If I am sin sick, then what I need is a physician, someone who understands the disease better than I do and who offers me medicine. That's Christ, or at least that's how I know him—bending over me in my pain, not condemning or punishing, but asking me to swallow bitter medicine.

•

I walked through the doors of that treatment center day after day and let God perform the surgery. I didn't try to understand it. The therapists gave me books and had me doing art and told me to light candles at night. *Just because they're nice*, one had said. I didn't do anything just because it was nice. But I went home and lit a candle. The staff gave me snacks when I wasn't hungry, and I ate them. They told me I couldn't exercise, so I didn't. There were worksheets and long talks and a dumb chaplain who told me that Catholics weren't Christian and who puffed up his chest about his MDiv when I challenged his outright ignorance. And there was a nurse who pissed me off with her desperate need to be needed by the patients, but none of that deterred me. Sometimes I wrestled, but mostly I had given up. That's what this kind of battle looks like. Resolute, painful surrender.

One day, I bought a used car. I walked onto the lot, pointed at one car, test drove it, signed the papers, and drove it home. The next day, when I met with the program psychiatrist, she laughed. She'd seen patients go on spending sprees, but no one had bought a car until now. *Well,* she said, *now you can take responsibility for your choices by paying it off for the next ten years.* My Volvo had finally coughed her last, but I didn't have twelve thousand dollars for a car. And so the car became an emblem of my stupidity. A frivolous thing I'd hitched myself to in a moment of unanswerable need. And she was right. The car followed me around, and I fed it what it needed—oil and gas and new tires—and made payments mostly on time, each one an installment against the long figurative and literal debt I owed.

•

In the late afternoons and evenings, I went to my classes and taught. I loved my students, who seemed sweetly innocent to me. Their words were plain and unpretentious. We read Larkin, Hughes and Kunitz, Angelou, Auden, Dickinson, and more. It was a feast. And when a line suddenly came together for them, randomness coalesced into meaning, and we rejoiced together. If they were bored, I didn't know it. It seemed to me that we had caught an updraft and were riding it.

•

When I couldn't run but needed to move, I went for long walks, down past the orange groves, past the blistered citrus and strip malls and tall ponderosa and the great, golden-domed Orthodox church I attended. I let the purpling sky work on me and the lifting cool, and when I wanted to scream or disappear or drink, I tapped my fingers against one another and made mental lists of Arctic animals, bodies of water, childhood toys. And sometimes, a poem came.

Those were the drains my writing circled in those days: the drain of wanting God but not feeling his presence, and the other, mysterious thought of an empty womb. I say mysterious because I did not actively want children, though perhaps I wanted what was signified by them—fruitfulness, stability, joy. I wanted to have the kind of life a child could live in without getting eaten. A lion and lamb sort of thing. Babe playing safely near an asp den. *Lord, let me be safe.*

•

Saint Andrew's was the church. Its gold glittered under the relentless sky. The pale stucco walls, domed Byzantine architecture, and a citrus grove across the street gave the impression of a church in Greece or Turkey.

But this was an American church led by an American priest who'd converted to Orthodoxy later in life. Inside, the ceilings were so high that the emptiness above my head felt heavy. And there were marble columns that stood like the trunks of primeval trees, and white marble floors, and everything echoed and felt ancient and remote. And I, standing in the back, felt lost in the sea of formal beauty and echo and austere, incandescent stone.

I went back and back, looking for God and sometimes catching him in an icon or the Eucharistic prayer or the Eucharist itself.

> Of thy Mystical Supper, O Son of God, accept me today as a communicant;
> . . . like the thief will I confess thee: Remember me, O Lord, in thy Kingdom.
> Not unto judgment nor unto condemnation be my partaking of thy Holy Mysteries,
> O Lord, but unto the healing of soul and body.

The words, *like the thief* and *unto the healing of soul and body*, sunk deep into my forking marrow and then rose out of me, as though they were my own words. *Remember me, O Lord, in thy Kingdom.* It was the desperate prayer of a desperate person, so far from God and hungry for that all-encompassing truth, the Man, whose eyes my eyes met across the belly of the church.

But the priest was a tall and severe person. And when he spoke, he often unknowingly ushered me toward the door. He hypothesized that family life in America nose-dived when women entered the workforce. Extramarital affairs, he claimed, could be blamed on this unfortunate development of modernity.

And he spoke with a whip about the problem of self-love. *The culture wants us to love ourselves!* he said as though outraged. *But that is not what Christ and his saints teach. They teach self-abasement. Self-hatred. If I am a Christian, I must hate myself and love only God.*

Sitting in a folding chair, I recoiled. Self-hatred was the water I swam in, and it was not particularly holy. And so instead of abandoning myself to the church, I set up a hedge, letting in some of the church, keeping other parts out. But who was I to judge? I, who was so recently given over to death? I did not want to analyze the church but to be raised up in her and by her—only the priest and his throng of zealous followers and their fervor and certainty got me twitching.

Some years later, I would be walking loops in a parking lot, kicking gravel and glancing up, from time to time, at a dark tree line. I was giving my confession to another priest, whom I trusted absolutely and whose love I loved. At the end my confession, he did not tell me to hate myself. *It's not a good word for everyone*, he said. *The church has many medicines, and some of them can make a person ill if they are given at the wrong time or for the wrong reason. Someday, the medicine of self-hatred might be good for you. But today, you must forget your sin. Can you see the face of Christ? That is all. Turn toward him. He has forgiven you and loves you. Now turn.*

•

Soon, treatment was done. Then school was over. I smoked a final cigarette with my recovery friends in a park, a little black dog happily licking our ankles. And we hugged and promised to keep in touch, and I meant it, despite what I knew about leaving people behind.

And I said goodbye to Kevin and the Texan and packed up my "responsibility" Honda. The overripe sun sat dripping on the western line as I drove off toward—God knew what. North again. Soon, the smell of green oranges faded. Then I turned on the radio and hung a foot out the window and let the wind in my hair and wondered if God hadn't meant for night to feel so good on the road.

# 16

# Mount Angel, Oregon

*There are days we live*
*as if death were nowhere*
*in the background; from joy*
*to joy to joy, from wing to wing,*
*from blossom to blossom to*
*impossible blossom, to sweet impossible blossom.*

Li Young Lee, "From Blossoms"

When I got sober that summer and for years afterward, my single, great hope was to just stay alive. Maybe I could get a job at a farm. Maybe I'd learn to paint. Maybe I could sponsor other women like me who suffered—not then, but later. And if none of that happened, who cared? I just wanted to be able to show up for my life. That by itself seemed an extravagant gift. Could I stand in it without flinching, letting the world be what it is, and letting myself be what I am?

•

After Riverside, there were moves and jobs. An engagement. A breakup.

At one point, I lived in a single-room cabin in the high desert of eastern Oregon for most of a year. The cabin was heated by a wood stove. There was a hot plate where I cooked and a loft bed near the roof, where the heat collected. I snuggled under layers of blankets and felt the emptiness of sage brush desert all around me and the sky and imagined my little poke of a cabin, and then I slept.

The cabin sat on a two-hundred-acre ranch, twenty-five minutes from Bend. In the mornings, I drove my responsibility car to work in town, and at night, when temperatures dropped below zero, I drove the dark, icy roads home and ran inside with my headlamp on and threw off my high heels and lit a fire and huddled near its iron belly until the cabin warmed.

There was a creek out back with snow and yellow dead grass on either bank. And geese flew sometimes in the gray frozen air, and I imagined all the icy grit in their wings, and the warm tubes of their throats as they honked.

And I ran the snow-packed roads with a giant dog named Bear and saw whole trees wrapped in ice and the morning light bursting through.

That would have been enough.

•

I worked a lot with teenagers in those days. Confused kids. Smart kids. Hurting kids. And I loved them. And I tried to seem cooler than I was because I thought that was the kind of authority they respected. But really, I think they were just grateful for someone who laughed at their jokes. And sometimes, in their pain, they wrote poems and read them to me.

And that would have been enough.

•

And then, one day, the light came back. I don't remember it happening. But there was a time light wasn't and then a time it was. And there's nothing more that can be said about that, except that the light wasn't me.

•

And what was lost came back. A good church with good people. A sane priest. And Christ was there, his steady eyes on my eyes, and he lit the fire in my belly again and breathed on it.

All of it would have been enough.

•

By the fall of 2015, I my quit my job (I'd been a teacher's aide in the autism room at a local public high school) and broke off an engagement and moved back to my parents' house. At home, I realized that Dad was declining. He left burners on so that all the pots blackened and kept signing up for scams and spent hours at his desk sorting and resorting the mail. Mom tried to tell the doctors that something had changed, but they shrugged it off. He's old, they said. It's normal.

I lived in the basement and emerged each day by midmorning to putter around the house with Dad. We went to Costco together, he in his khakis and flannel button-downs, and we chatted about what makes a good watch, and I used my mom's money to buy foods he liked, rice pudding and ice cream and bananas.

There was a part of me that thought I might end up like this forever—a girl who lives at home. No career. No life of my own. Restless, I smoked on the back porch and went to recovery meetings and read in the living room with Dad, though I'm not sure he read then so much as bowed his head and shuttled his eyes back and forth across the page. He'd spent his life like that, bent over books. I'm not sure he knew any other way to sit in a living room.

Then one day, my dad and I were standing at the kitchen sink looking out the window when a blue bird flashed a bright wing and disappeared. My dad pointed to where the wing had been and said, *The end of the century*. That blue, the end. Somehow it made sense to me.

That night, I opened my laptop and started looking up graduate programs where my favorite poets taught. I wanted poetry again, but something more this time. I wanted poetry and God. I wanted to learn from people who pressed the ache of necessity and light into language and could show me how.

So I knocked on a few doors. Yale, Notre Dame, University of Missouri. If none of them opened, what would I have lost? $150 in application fees? Then I could go back to watching my dad's slow death and the empty hydrangea stems, winter morning light through curtains and electric moss blooming the sidewalk. And I could cook oatmeal for him every morning. And in the afternoon we would talk about death as though it had already happened, as though it walked with us down the street under the tall Douglas fir.

•

Surprisingly, a few of those doors opened. And so, in 2016 I kissed my confused father and overtired mother goodbye and boarded a plane with my cat and two suitcases and flew to New York. It was 2016 when I traveled by Uber and train to New Haven, Connecticut.

And it was 2016 when I found the beautiful stone residential college where my half brother, Greg, had lived as physics major in the '80s. 2016 when I stepped foot in my first class at Yale, quivering with the promise of it all.

Of course, it was beautiful. New England beautiful. Tall trees, the open green, bridges. But more than anything, more than anywhere I'd lived before, there was a kind of *human* beauty. Buildings filled with art. Chamber music. Libraries that looked like castles. The beauty of human labor rose up and spread a great wing over the city, or at least the university campus. Outside Yale's rarefied bubble, houses grew increasingly small, then there were broken sidewalks and cheap nail salons and bars on windows.

Though I was conscious of the distance between the broken sidewalk and the stone archway through which I walked to class, and though the distance whispered at the unreality of my comfort, I let myself be taken in and up. *Just a taste*, I told myself. *Then I'll let myself back down into the hard world.*

My professors were brilliant and engaged and rigorous. I read Dante and didn't mind too much that I wasn't very good at Italian poetry. And there were classes on the church fathers, Saint Irenaeus and Origen and Saint Gregory Nazianzen. And we read religious poets and the mystics and medieval theologians. I spent the whole first year dizzy and swooning and lapping what I could from the overflow. One professor laughed when I told him how wonderful I found it all. *Yes*, he said. *An embarrassment of riches.*

•

And in that golden time, I met golden friends, mostly women, mostly younger than me. Bright-witted, earnest women steeped in Protestant Christian theology, stepping out for the first time into the great ocean of Christian tradition, its historical and creative depth. The dead sang to us that year, as we talked about Mary and sacramental life and the twin rigors of Christianity—heart and mind—and how lacking one a church might wilt or calcify.

In the fog of morning, we hiked stubborn, old hills. Sheer mist against our faces. And the maples rose high and orange in the canopy. Maple and white birch and Norway spruce, each fanning their obstinate limbs against the falling year. Soon, snow. But for now, gold leaves fluttered in the wind. Sometimes we were silent, sometimes we breathed aloud our wonder over a carpet of soft coins.

•

Then snow did come, and I stomped up and down Prospect Hill in my snow boots. And I memorized lines of poems as I walked thirty minutes to class in the morning. Then thirty minutes home in the evening. I did not go with the other students to bars and instead went to recovery meetings or home to my cat. And at home I ate without excess and did not starve myself and enjoyed my toast with peanut butter in the mornings and my French press and my chair and the lamp and everything plain and uncomplicated and full of peace. My mind unburdened by warfare, I was able to take in the soft curve of the cat's body in my lap, the *Aeneid* open to my side.

•

The next year I moved closer to the divinity school. A three-bedroom apartment sat on top of an Italian restaurant. And across the street there was a little Italian market. Three markets, in fact. All Italian, all selling fresh vegetables and little sweets and sausages and tins of coffee. Later I learned that in the beginning there had been one Italian shop, but then a family disagreement resulted in a split. So, a few blocks down the road another Italian market popped opened. Of course, it was only a matter of time before tensions rose again, and when they did Orange Street was crowned with its third Italian market. One of the markets was known for sandwiches. Another for cheap prices. Another for sweets.

The stairwell up to my apartment smelled like tomatoes and garlic and fresh-baked bread. And at the top, there were my friends. Two women, each lovely and good and interesting to talk to.

•

Once, when I was cooking eggs in the kitchen, my spatula hand stopped midair and I was gone for a second, two, three. Memory's like that, hidden all around. Tap on the door. Walk past the sign. Look right. Look left. Suddenly the smell of boots. The forgotten feeling swoops in, the past suddenly all there is.

That day an old, black feeling shuttered out the eggs frying in front of me. A portal had opened and sucked me far away from the morning's gentle satisfactions, far out into urgency, war, apocalypse. My old unit was marching down a wet asphalt road. The smell of gun oil and rubber and rain. The feel of damp BDUs stuck to my arms. The collective movement. *Right, oh right, oh right, left, right.*

*Nine to the front, six to the rear. That's the way we do it here.* Where were we going?

Then it was gone, and I startled back. The eggs were burned. My spatula hand lowered. And I felt my way back into life. That's when I realized how strange the contrast. The girl carrying an M16 could not have imagined the girl remembering her now. And with pity and remorse I remembered the sense of death's proximity and dominion.

•

The laundry machine was in the basement of the house next door. Our landlady owned both properties, so we had a key to the basement and walked down the rickety steps and put our coins in the machines to clean our clothes.

One day, I was reading in the living room when I remembered a load of clothes I'd left in the washer too long. I dropped the book and hurried out into the autumn chill to change them over. I think I might have been swearing as I opened the door and stomped down the wooden stairs and making such a ruckus I almost didn't see the person standing in front of the washer.

But at last I did see him—a tall, handsome, bearded man wearing a black T-shirt and holding up a fistful of my wet clothes. He laughed at me, when he saw me with my hat almost falling off. And then we introduced ourselves and exchanged a few jokes. What did he say? But it doesn't matter. I liked him right away and from that moment on kept an eye out for the tall guy swooping around campus in a black navy trench coat.

The next semester, I noticed he was in my Augustine seminar. He sat in the back and was very quiet, which made him seem brilliant. Later, he told me that he'd noticed me too, though he wouldn't say *what* he'd noticed.

It could have just as easily never happened. Not *as* easily. It would have been far easier for us to have never met, let alone dated. Graham was a very satisfied loner in those days. And indecisive. But one night, he asked if he could bum a cigarette, and so we stood on the back porch of his house and smoked and talked. It turned out he had been a car mechanic before he went to community college. He still loved to work with his hands, even though he didn't think he was especially good at it. Then he'd gone on to study philosophy first as an undergraduate, then as a graduate student in England. All of it, he said, had to do with God. It had never been his plan to become a priest, but here he was, halfway to ordination. He said all of that slowly, over the course of maybe an hour with jokes and silence in between.

I saw his face in the half-light of the moon and leaned in close enough to get a sense for him, some animal quality that added its own *yes* to the chorus already sounding. And somehow I knew, or wanted to know, what we would become.

•

It was spring. That's all I remember. My head didn't work right. Love drunk. The dogwoods in full bloom, white and pink petals everywhere. One April day, Graham and I read on a blanket spread out under the high branches of a tree in the park until a rainstorm dumped buckets on us. We ran back to his house soaking wet and laughing, and I kissed him, and we smelled like spring to one another, something fresh and clean and lovely.

•

That summer, Henry got married. And so, less than two months after our first date, Graham flew out to Oregon and met my entire family.

Henry was not a meth addict anymore. He hadn't let a mind-altering chemical past the gateway of his mouth for over thirteen years. And somehow over those thirteen years, he'd become an earnest Catholic and gotten into a prestigious law school. That's where he'd met Emma, in a Hyde Park recovery meeting. She was just a few years sober, a beautiful, brilliant med student. But most importantly, she didn't take any of Henry's shit and wasn't impressed by him, which made him adore her. They fell in love in the stupid way we all do, and happily it stuck. In June 2018, they were married in a Catholic church in Oregon. And all our family danced and cheered and no one was sad that day. Dad, especially, though his mind was further from us than ever, wept and clapped his hands. And I stood with him and put my arm around his waist and watched his boy, my brother, walk hand in hand with a good woman before God.

•

A few days later, Dad was driving home from Costco when he fell asleep. Or something like sleep came over him. And he drove off the road and through a ditch into someone's fence.

He was fine but confused. The police revoked his license after that, or at least that's what Mom told him. And so he started gathering papers at home, evidence of his competence. Once he got the papers together, I was going to drive him to the police station, and they would return his license. But the papers never came together; they scattered and then found piles and then blew apart and re-formed. Bills and old letters and a few photos of his parents, which he studied with a magnifying glass, over and over.

I decided to stay the summer to help take care of Dad. Mom had been trying to care for him while working full-time and was struggling. Sometimes, Dad would pack a brown grocery sack with socks and announce that he needed to go home to his parents' house. He didn't know why he was here. And he would jiggle the doorknob and look out the large front windows and sometimes cry for the street where his dead parents lived.

Mom and I didn't contradict him. *Yes, we will take you to your parents soon. But your mom asked us to feed you dinner first. Can we eat dinner before we leave? She would like that.* He spoke a lot about a committee that made decisions for him and asked him to perform different tasks around the house, like laying out banana peels on napkins. So, sometimes it was helpful to invoke the authority of the committee if we needed to get something done. *Dad, the committee has asked you to put on your socks so we can go for a walk. They put it in a memo this morning. Shall we put on your socks?*

Once, walking down the street, I saw a piece of wood with worm trails etched into its side and thought of my father's brain. Dad, standing in a cold shower believing he was dead. Dad, pointing to a half-dead worm on the sidewalk and shouting, *Life!*

Once, a staple gun sounded rhythmically in the distance. Bang, bang, bang. A new coffee shop was going up. Dad turned to Mom and said, *It's quiet here except for the executions.* She didn't laugh then but when she told me later, we laughed until we cried.

But as the shower and worm and staple gun grew in violence, Dad became a gentler man, a sweet and funny rabbit of a man, a person he never or always was. He loved children especially and children's books and was happy to hug and kiss us. Even though I knew it was because the worm was eating his mind, I was strangely happy for his heart—unburdened, at last.

•

Graham and I married the next summer. We lived in a tiny house in Oklahoma and played tennis badly in the afternoons, when the sun hovered fat and indolent over the court. Graham had been ordained a priest in the Oklahoma diocese and served at a beautiful, thriving church. And though I pined for Orthodoxy, I went to the church where my husband celebrated the mysteries and preached. I was learning to love God in a new key—a Western key that had not been the sound of my prayer for many years.

Before our first anniversary, we had a son. A bright leaf of fire. A beautiful person. The most beautiful I'd ever seen. Born near Pentecost and red-headed in June. Hands in fists, eyes new to light.

That little home is where we learned about love—sleepless, anxious love, love that violently hews a person's heart and tucks the ones you love deep into the wound. Red body of child, tiny on his father's broad chest or against the cushion of mine. And cicadas sang their brief song, and the red dirt grew almost nothing, and Graham's tomato plants wilted out back. But our boy grew, and when he was seven months old, the three of us got on a plane taking us to Oregon. It was time.

•

He had days, the nurse told us. Maybe two or three. Dad was lying on a hospital bed set up in the TV room in my parents' house. Henry and Emma had been there for a few days already. A priest had said last rites, had prayed and given him a final Eucharist, the last thing my dad ever ate. *Food for the journey*, the priest had said.

We arrived full of travel and forward movement and fluster. And then we were inside, where everything seemed to have stopped, the whole house still. And there was my dad. Graham put a hand on Dad's shoulder and bowed his head and then took the baby into the living room.

The mind bounces off death like a rubber ball. There was my dad's face, hollow-cheeked, close-eyed. But what my eyes saw, the mind rejected, skipping over the thing it couldn't understand. So it was another part of me that sat by Dad's side and held his hand and wept and kissed him. Until finally I said, *I'd like to go skiing with you again, Dad.* And he groaned and lifted his hand, as though to say something like, *Yes.* It was our last conversation.

Over the next days, the nurse came by regularly to check on him. He was supposed to pass quickly. No food or water now. Only ice chips and morphine.

But he didn't die. Days passed. Then a week. We spent most of our days gathered around him. Sometimes we sang hymns. Sometimes we prayed over him. Sometimes we told stories or talked about the news or work or teased one another. At night, we kept vigil. I got through the Gospel of Luke with him that way, a candle flickering next to flowers, a tissue box. But still, he didn't die. The nurse said she didn't know how he persisted. It didn't make medical sense.

I didn't want him to die, but I wanted the waiting to stop. Our hearts stretched out. Except for the baby, who was fat and sweet-eyed and demanded so much concrete attention, I would have lost myself on the rack of grief. Here was joy, the beautiful soft curve of my son's tummy, his dirty diaper, his sticky hand around my finger. His life was so much more life than any of ours. Two poles. Wax, wane. Breath and ash.

The only one absent was Greg, Dad's first child. Mom had let him know that Dad was dying, but Greg didn't want to come. He'd fly out for the funeral, he'd said. And that was that.

On the tenth day, in that strained and sleep-deprived state, it occurred to me that Dad might be waiting to say goodbye. The nurse had mentioned that sort of thing happening. So I called Greg. Dad had been in a coma for a week. No water or food for ten days. I got Greg's voicemail and left a message and went upstairs to put the baby down for a nap.

While I was gone, Greg called back. Mom answered my phone and held it up to Dad's ear. Greg, estranged son and devout atheist said: *I love you, Dad. You can go now.* Then a few breaths later. *I'll see you on the other side, Dad.*

When Mom looked down, Dad was gone. Mouth open and empty.

•

That was death. No one tore their hair out. When I came downstairs, Henry and Mom were weeping and the room was full of light. Graham told me what had happened, and while the baby slept, I cried out inexplicably, *Hallelujah, hallelujah.* I wasn't sure what I meant by it, but it didn't matter. It was the only word.

Death came into the house but had no foothold. Dad died. Just not in the way any of us expected. There was so much more life than death. How conquered it seemed then. So small in the wake of what filled the room, like wings. And we who loved Dad, we who could have just as easily been high or drunk or numb, were awake to see it.

•

After we chose the coffin—nothing ornate, nothing undignified, nothing that suggested much more than a nap—and Dad's body was laid in it. After he was solemnly marched to the front of the Catholic church, under the high ceiling, under candlelight and the monks' low prayers, under the word of God, the word he finally hung his life on, after that we ate cucumber sandwiches in Mom's backyard (it was only hers now). I remember light tunneling through us painfully. And there was Mom nodding abstractly as a stranger spoke to her about golf. And there were friends who had shown up. Their faces seem so beautiful to me now, those women who came and held my baby and did not ask me to tell them about my grief.

After everyone left, Graham picked up our son, and we wandered out past the fence and stood a while under a huge, old walnut tree. For a brief moment the world fuzzed. Graham put the boy down in the grass of Nineveh. There was a small, dying church across a field. Cobwebs in the fallen branches near our feet. Have you ever seen a walnut in spring? The green rind rotted off, the fibrous husk exposed from the wet winter. Despite decay, the seed is often still good. I watched my boy, all soft cream and bright eyes, find one and bend his head over it. Make of it what you will, but the husk fell apart in his hands, wet and dark as good earth, and he put the bright seed to his mouth.

Acknowledgments

Without the help, support, and encouragement of countless people this book would not exist. Thank you, first, to the many friends of Bill who welcomed me, loved me, and told me the truth. I only get to live the life I have now because of you.

And to all of you who prayed over this book, that it would become the book God had in mind. I have no doubt that you are responsible for whatever truth this book contains.

And to the long-suffering saints who read and commented on early drafts: Jenny Williams, Abby Anderson, Amber Noel, and James Kilcup. Your friendship and readerly insights were and are a gift.

Many thanks to my agent, Don Pape, who took a chance on representing an unknown, middle-aged mom living in Oklahoma. You've been a true friend and advocate of this work.

And to my editors, Lisa Ann Cockrel and Laurel Draper. Your keen observations, clarity of vision, and deep understanding of both the mechanics and music of language played a pivotal role in the development and refinement of this book. Thank you.

For their encouragement, patience, and honesty, I'd like to thank Fr. Dan Suciu, Fr. Stephen Soot, Fr. Theodore Dorrance, Anna Keesey, Lex Runciman, Katie Ford, Andrew Winer, Dr. Andrew McGowan, Dr. Peter Hawkins, and Christian Wiman. In small ways and large, you prodded me along the path.

And to my mom, the person who ignited my passion for language, who has loved me through it all, and who generously read many drafts of this book with an expansive heart and sharp editorial eye. I love you.

My deepest thanks go to my husband, my dearest friend and champion. You believed in this book long before I did and encouraged me along the way. You watched the children on your days off so I could steal precious hours away from home. You changed the oil in my car and steadied my anxious heart. After the good Lord, you and the boys are the chief blessing of my life. For this and more, I'm grateful.

And finally, thank you to my father, Rodney Weston Kilcup, who was and is a giant of goodness in my life. His love, sober virtue, laughter, and error walk around my life like living friends. Even now, he hovers like a searching bird as I write, asking, *Have you said the central thing?* See you on the other side, Dad.

# Notes

xi **The ocean is stratified into five layers** I use the colloquial names for the five oceanic zones, but they are properly known as the epipelagic zone, the mesopelagic zone, the bathypelagic zone, the abyssopelagic zone, and the hadalpelagic zone. "Layers of the Ocean," National Oceanic and Atmospheric Administration, updated March 28, 2023, https://www.noaa.gov/jetstream/ocean/layers-of-ocean.

xiii ***Synonym: ambivalence of the human heart (see: Jonah)*** This poem modifies the *Online Dictionary* definition of "violence." "Violence," *Online Dictionary*, accessed June 11, 2024, https://www.dictionary.com/browse/violence.

3 **2008 market crash** For more information on unemployment rates after the market crash of 2008, see Arne L. Kalleberg and Till M. von Wachter, "The U.S. Labor Market During and After the Great Recession: Continuities and Transformations," *RSF: The Russell Sage Foundation Journal of the Social Sciences* 3, no. 3 (2017): 1–19, https://doi.org/10.7758/rsf.2017.3.3.01.

7 **"A beautiful woman looking at her image in the mirror"** Simone Weil, *Gravity and Grace* (University of Nebraska Press, 1997), 79.

11 **Orthodox art** For more information on iconography in the Orthodox tradition, see Fr. Maximos Constas, *The Art of Seeing: Paradox and Perception in Orthodox Iconography* (Sebastian Press, 2014).

16 **MEPS** Military Entrance Processing Station.

**the ASVAB** This military acronym stands for Armed Services Vocational Aptitude Battery. The multisubject test is used to sort potential soldiers, sailors, marines, and airmen into jobs.

**DLAB** A language-learning test.

22 **CERN** The European Organization for Nuclear Research, an international particle physics research laboratory in Geneva, Switzerland.

28 **Like Anselmo, I hated the idea of war** Anselmo is a character in Ernest Hemmingway's novel *For Whom the Bell Tolls* (Charles Scribner's Sons, 1940). A devout Catholic, Anselmo expresses moral aversion to war but dutifully fights alongside the Republicans in the Spanish Civil War out of a sense of civic responsibility.

32 **One of our favorite stories . . . was about a newly married couple** This was the story as my dad told it, but the no-less-dramatic true story of Adeana Dickinson's death can be found in the *Anchorage Daily News*. Apparently, Adeana and Jay were newlyweds, but she wasn't posing for a picture in her wedding dress. They were riding an ATV, which got stuck in the mud. When Adeana tried to push it out, the mud started sucking her down. Her husband and a state trooper stayed with her until the tide came in. See David Reamer, "The True Story of Cook Inlet's Deadly Mudflats," *Anchorage Daily News*, July 13, 2020, https://www.adn.com/alaska-life/2020/07/13/the-true-history-of-cook-inlets-deadly-mudflats/.

41 **BDU** Battle dress uniform. It's what everyone pictures soldiers wearing—green and brown camo, big cargo pockets, tall black, lace-up boots.

**"chipped pavement and weedy lots and junk heaps"** John Steinbeck, *Cannery Row* (Viking, 1945), 1.

42 **PT uniforms** Physical training (exercise) uniforms.

43 ***Gde toofli? . . . Tam na polu.*** Russian, meaning, "Where are the shoes?" . . . "There, on the floor."

45 **Saint Mary of Egypt** For more information, read the hagiography "Venerable Mary of Egypt," Orthodox Church in America, accessed August 7, 2025, https://www.oca.org/saints/lives/2025/04/01/100963-venerable-mary-of-egypt.

61 **catechumens** in the Orthodox Church, laypeople who attend an Orthodox church but have not yet been sacramentally received into the church by baptism or chrysmation. Orthodox catechumens typically spend at least a year attending church services and catechetical classes in order to prepare for full membership in the church.

62 **as Saint Irenaeus put it** In *Against Heresies*, book 4, Saint Irenaeus writes, "The glory of God is man fully alive." By "man," Irenaeus meant Christ and by extension all people whose lives are Christ's, Christ being life itself, the life we are meant to be filled by.

**The desert authors of the eight deadly thoughts** Mary Margaret Funk describes the desert authors' eight deadly thoughts in *Thoughts Matter: The Practice of the Spiritual Life* (Continuum, 1998).

**"The things you think about determine the quality of your mind"** Marcus Aurelius, *Meditations* 5.16.

78 **the *Left Behind*** The *Left Behind* movies were based on a series of apocalyptic/eschatological novels written in the 1990s by Tim LaHaye and Jerry B. Jenkins. Based on the New Testament book of Revelation, these fictional books were frequently read in evangelical and fundamentalist circles as literal renderings of the post-rapture future.

83 **PLDC** The Primary Leadership Development Course, a month-long training program for enlisted soldiers who were either about to be or had recently been promoted to the rank of sergeant, the lowest leadership rank in the Army.

102 **ETS date** Expiration Term of Service date.

111 **Mount Athos** Mount Athos is an ancient site of Christian monastic life. Monks are known to have inhabited the Grecian peninsula as early as the fourth century, though formal monastic communities didn't appear for another several centuries. The "Holy Mountain," as it is called, continues to be a center of Orthodox spiritual life and teaching today.

117 **The word "bulimia" comes from Greek** "Bulimia," *Etymology Online*, accessed November 1, 2024, https://www.etymonline.com/word/bulimia.

119 **"As kingfishers catch fire, dragonflies draw flame"** Gerard Manley Hopkins, "When Kingfishers Catch Fire."

127 **a book by Orthodox Hieromonk Gregorios** Hieromonk Gregorios, *Repentance and Confession* (Newrome Press, 2015).

146 **"Almighty God, Father of our Lord Jesus Christ"** "Holy Communion," *Book of Common Prayer* (1928), 75.

150 **"God, I offer myself to thee"** *Alcoholics Anonymous*, 4th ed. (Alcoholics Anonymous World Service, 2013), 63.

# About the Author

After high school, Kathleen Kilcup spent five years serving in the US Army as a Russian linguist. In addition to her time as a soldier, she has worked as a janitor, a wildland firefighter, an editor, a barista, a farm hand, a landscaper, a nonprofit program director, a chocolate maker, a writing tutor, and a factory worker.

She earned an MFA in poetry from UC Riverside and an MA in religion and arts from Yale Divinity School. Her poetry and essays address matters of faith, addiction, motherhood, mental illness, work, gender, and prayer. *Rough Hymns*, her first poetry chapbook, was published in 2018 by Finishing Line Press.

Kilcup has lived in ten states and two countries and traveled to many more. She is now happily rooted in the suburbs of Oklahoma City where she lives with her husband and two children.

Text set in Garamond Premier, designed by Robert Slimbach

Cover design: HD Brewer
Book design: Lydia Christine Hall
Proofreader: Rachel Martens
Copyeditor: Laurel Draper
Acquiring editor: Lisa Ann Cockrel

Here Below champions ambitious books that eschew binaries between the sacred and profane. Learn more at herebelowbooks.com.